THE NFL
SUPER BOWL
COMPANION

THE

SUPER

COMP

TRIUMPH
B O O K S
CHICAGO

NFL
BOWL
ANION

EDITED BY JOHN WIEBUSCH

CONTENTS

All *38 pieces in* The NFL Super Bowl Companion *originally appeared in Super Bowl Game Programs, beginning with Bill McGrane's "Ready...or Not" in Super Bowl XXII. Most articles here have not been updated but rather appear as they were written, with the program in which they appeared noted at the start of the piece.*

DAVE BARRY

THAT'S MY BOY

A keen-eyed football observation from
humorist Dave Barry: The bigger they
are, the more easily they win

FROM SUPER BOWL XXXIII

I T'S LATE OCTOBER, and I'm watching my son play football. Well, okay, he's not technically playing. He's on the sidelines, number 85, standing near the coach, looking alert, hoping the coach will notice him and send him in. I'm not so sure this is a good idea because the other team's players are extremely large. They're supposed to be junior-high students, but if they are, they apparently started junior high later in life, after having played a number of years for the Chicago Bears. They look extremely mature. You can actually see their beards growing. They probably have to shave in the huddle.

In stark contrast, my son's team, the Raiders, consists of normal-sized seventh- and eighth-grade boys, except for player number 9, Nicole, who is a girl. From a distance, with their helmets and shoulder pads on, the Raiders look big enough, but this illusion is shattered when you see them up close, or when one of their moms walks past, towering over them.

For some reason the Raiders' opponents always are larger. Also, they seem more aggressive. They punch each other a lot and spit and sneer and probably eat live chickens on the team bus. Also, they're always gathering together and emitting loud, menacing, unintelligible football roars, whereas the Raiders tend to chat. The Raiders are a more laid-back group. Sometimes they try to make a menacing football roar, but it comes out sounding halfhearted, like a group throat clearing.

This is the Raiders' sixth game. So far they've won one; that victory was sealed when the opposing team, in what has proved to be the Raiders' season highlight so far, failed to show up. The Raiders lost all the other games, in large part because...at least this is how I analyze the situation from a strictly technical standpoint...they have not scored any points.

Usually, when the Raiders have the ball, giant live-chicken-eating Chicago Bears knock them down and take it away. Whereas when the opponents have the ball, they give it to some enormous player who cannot possibly be in junior high school because any given one of his calves is larger than a junior high school. This player lumbers toward the plucky Raiders defenders, who leap up and latch on to him, one after the other, until the runner is lumbering down the field with what appears to be the entire Raiders defensive unit clinging desperately to his body, the whole group looking like some bizarre alien space creature with many extra heads and arms and legs and two really huge calves.

On the sidelines, we grownups yell helpful advice.

"Tackle him!" shouts a Raiders coach. "Somebody tackle him!"

"Bite his ankles!" shouts a man.

Inevitably, the Chicago Bears score a touchdown, causing us Raiders parents to groan. The Raiders cheerleaders, however, remain undaunted. They have a cheer for just this situation. It goes (I am not making this cheer up):

"They made a touchdown!

"But it's all right!"

The Raiders cheerleaders remain perky and upbeat no matter what happens in the game. They face us parents, going through their routines, happy in their own totally separate cheerleading world. A plane could crash on the field and they might not notice, and even if they did, I bet it wouldn't seriously impact their perkiness ("A plane crashed on the field! But it's all right!")

Of course, they have good reason to be cheerful. They're in no danger of being converted into gridiron roadkill by the Chicago Bears. My son, on the other hand, is...

My son is going into the game.

The coach is telling him something. I hope it's good advice (such as "Tennis is a much safer sport."). And now number 85 is trotting onto the field; and now he's taking his position on the Raiders' defensive line; and now both teams are lined up; and now my son is crouching down in his stance, ready to spring forward...

THERE HE GOES! GET 'EM, ROB! STICK YOUR HELMET COMPLETELY THROUGH SOME BIG FAT CHICAGO BEARS BODY AND OUT THE OTHER SIDE! YES! WAY TO GO! WAY TO POUNCE! WAY TO BE...

Offside. Whoops.

Okay, so he was a little overeager. But he did fine after that, as far as I could tell, lunging around out there just like everybody else and managing to go four full plays without once losing an important limb or organ. Another positive note was that Nicole got into the game and was actually sort of involved in a tackle.

But that was pretty much the highlight for the Raiders, who became increasingly resigned and philosophical as it became clear that they were going to lose yet again. Meanwhile, the Chicago Bears, feeling smug, were emitting fierce victory grunts.

"I BET OUR S.A.T. SCORES ARE HIGHER," I wanted to yell. But, of course, I did not, as I prefer not to have my head stomped into pudding.

Finally the game ended, and even though the Raiders again failed to score any points, we parents were tremendously proud. We clapped and cheered with pride as they trotted off the field.

They think we're crazy.

JIM ARMSTRONG

DA TEAM OF DESTINY

No football team, before or since,

was quite as outrageous as the

Super Bowl XX champion Bears

FROM SUPER BOWL XXXVI

I T WAS 2:30 in the morning, barely 40 hours before Super Bowl XX, and the Danimal was sneaking in one last strategy session on Bourbon Street. As he talked Dos Equis and Os with his new best friends, someone asked Bears defensive tackle Dan Hampton why their fearless leader, quarterback Jim McMahon, wasn't there to receive his perfect-attendance citation for the week.

"Everybody's going, 'What's the deal with McMahon? Is he okay?' I told them, 'Calm down, he'll be fine. He may be off his rocker, but there's a method to his madness. He's probably in bed right now with his playbook tucked under his pillow,'" says Hampton. "No sooner had I said it, fifty people walk in and McMahon is in the middle of them. He's wearing a headband, with neon lights, his eyeballs are falling out, he's got three beers in each hand, and he's wearing a T-shirt that says 'Patriots Suck.' Everybody looked

9

at me and I said, 'Well, maybe I don't know what's going on after all.'"

Figures. Even if you were one of them, you never knew quite what to expect from those 1985 Bears. Unless, of course, it was Sunday. Then you knew. Da Bears didn't just beat you. They broke your spirit, crushed your confidence, bruised your ribs, and left footprints on your facemask. Then they threw your quarterback into the nose-bleed section. But first, just to be fair, they told you they were going to do it. Advertised it in a video, in fact. Or don't you remember the "Super Bowl Shuffle," that time-tested testament to trash talking the players produced in early December, seven weeks before arriving in New Orleans?

"People ask me how much we intimidated teams," says linebacker Mike Singletary. "I kid you not, there were points in games when I literally got the guys in the huddle and said, 'Hey, don't hit 'em again, don't hit 'em like that. They've had enough.' I saw quarterbacks crying. I saw running backs trembling. I saw linemen who wanted to leave. I could see it in their eyes. We had hired assassins on that team. I mean they could take you out."

And when they were done, they would grab their brushes and red paint and head for town. They sucked the juices out of life, but only if a half-keg wasn't handy. They walked the walk, talked the talk, and prowled the prowl. They were young and restless, bold and brash, loud and proud. They were uncouth, unkempt, unabashed, and all but unbeatable. Their unofficial team mascot was perpetually-disheveled comedian Bill Murray, who never met a man he didn't like. Provided, of course, the guy was buying. Murray would crack the players up during the playoffs with his eyes-glaring, arms-folded, gum-smacking imitation of Da Coach, Mike Ditka.

They were a unique bunch, those 1985 Bears. Only Da Bears could have inspired a *Saturday Night Live* skit. Only Da Bears could have had a gap-toothed 340-pound defensive tackle who doubled as a fullback, an athlete so gifted he could dunk a basketball, a personality so bubbly he became a folk hero. Only Da Bears could have had a quarterback who head butted teammates and butted heads with the league office, and who constantly wore sunglasses, as one Chicago columnist wrote, "so as not to be affected by any sunlight reflecting off his close friend, the beer can." Only Da Bears could have had a coach whose many moods prompted the players to nickname him Sybil, a coach who, for the most part, talked to his defensive coordinator only when the other team scored. In other words, every other week or so.

"They were characters on that team, but they had character," says Ditka. "The one thing we didn't try to do was rein them in. I didn't fine them a lot. I let the little stuff go, the petty things, because they got their work done. We didn't have any ego problems because we hadn't won anything. We were climbing the mountain. I've never seen a team have as much fun as that one. You know, I cut a pretty good swath as a player, too. We left a few buildings standing on Rush Street, and those guys knocked them down."

Yep, they were one, big happy family, those '85 Bears. Of course, so were the Mansons. There were more personalities in the locker room than waves in nearby Lake Michigan. You had the Danimal, Mongo, the Fridge, Sweetness, and Da Coach. You had Singletary, the steely-eyed man in the middle, the devout Christian who made ball carriers pray for mercy. You had McMahon, the wild man in the headband whose body belonged in the Smithsonian. You had Buddy Ryan, the cantankerous defensive coordinator whose brainstorm, the 46 defense, forever changed the way the game is played. Oh, and let's not forget Richard Dent, the should-be Hall of Fame defensive end whose surname was derived from what he inflicted on quarterbacks. Hampton, also a Canton candidate who moonlighted as the keeper of the nicknames, dubbed Dent the Colonel. Why the Colonel? Because, like Harland Sanders, he did one thing, and he did it right.

"The analogy in the movies would be *It's a Mad, Mad, Mad, Mad World*," says Hampton. "We could carouse with the best of them. We led the league in breaking curfew, but we didn't have knuckleheads who got into fights and got arrested and that stuff. We were nuts, but there was a lot of love in that locker room. No backbiting, no jealousy, nothing. It was all a complete team effort. A lot of times, the greatest stories in life are by happenstance. You couldn't script the stuff that happened on that team. We weren't trying to impress somebody like a Dennis Rodman. It wasn't like anything was premeditated. We just had several dynamic personalities and, for that one shining season, all the pieces fell together. It was our Magical Mystery Tour."

"I've been around this world a lot, and I've never come across that many characters in that small a space at one time," says defensive tackle Steve (Mongo) McMichael. "We entertained each other. We had a bunch of guys who liked to have fun. We spent the whole season laughing at each other. But we had a serious side, too. When it was time to whip somebody's butt, we did it. We were like an engine with different parts all working together. People will always remember that team, but you know what? If we had lost, nobody would have remembered. We backed it up. We don't have to claim fame, brother. We achieved it."

What made the '85 Bears unique was that they predicted it. They didn't talk the talk so much as scream it at the top of their lungs. And they didn't care if their doors were open, closed, or ajar at the time. They were a team for the ages, and they knew it at that moment, as it was unfolding, long before the confetti flew in New Orleans. With apologies to Walter Payton, the most prolific running back in NFL history, and McMahon, who didn't throw an interception in three postseason games, it came down to defense. There had never been anything like it in the blocking-and-tackling business. The Bears' 46 defense, with its eight-man fronts and relentless pass rush, shut out the Giants in a divisional playoff game, then shut out the Rams in the NFC Championship Game. The wonder is how the Patriots ever scored 10 points in the Super Bowl, what with their offense backpedaling for minus-19 yards in the first half.

A lot of it was talent, of course. The Bears' front office had enjoyed an incredible run on draft day to set up that '85 season. In the six previous years, the Bears had used eight number-one draft choices to select Hampton, Al Harris, Otis Wilson, Keith Van

Horne, McMahon, Jimbo Covert, Willie Gault, and Wilber Marshall. It was a matter of talent, all right. And attitude. Lots and lots of attitude. Da Bears won because they knew they could not lose. Sure, they had their issues. McMahon always seemed to be on the trainer's table, and Ryan and Ditka, a marriage forced by Papa Bear, owner George Halas, never saw eye to eye. But nothing was going to stop the Bears from fulfilling their destiny, and they knew it.

"Believe me, we led the league in arrogance," says Hampton. "We had great confidence. We had spent the last half of the season just waiting for the playoffs. It wasn't just the players. We're going into the NFC Championship Game, and we've got a defensive coordinator talking trash. Buddy says, 'We'll shut 'em out, and Eric Dickerson will fumble three times.' Well guess what happens? He fumbled twice, and we shut 'em out. It's the old Dizzy Dean thing. It ain't bragging if you can back it up."

Says Ryan, "None of that stuff bothered me. We were always predicting somebody would fumble three times. I came up with the Jets, and I was there when Joe Namath guaranteed a win in the Super Bowl. To me, it showed a lot of confidence. Intimidating people is all part of it, and I know we intimidated teams. They were afraid of that defense. We played the Raiders the year before in Chicago. When the Raiders leave town and say you're the dirtiest team they've ever played, you know you've arrived."

The Bears' players knew long before the Super Bowl that they had something special on their hands. But the fact was, they hadn't won a conference championship, much less a Super Bowl, so they couldn't be sure they had the right stuff. Until November 17, that is. That's when they traveled to Dallas to play the Cowboys, proud owners of the league's most enduring mystique, not to mention some of the NFL's best talent. For the Bears, that game was the closing argument. Win it and nothing could stand in their path.

"We're 10-0 and they're 7-3, but they're the ones talking," says Hampton. "Everson Walls says, 'Yeah, yeah, but they ain't played anybody.' Ditka had coached in Dallas, and Singletary, McMichael, and I had all played in the Southwest Conference. That was the big game for us. If they beat us, we were all a big puff balloon. We had played them in the preseason, and there were a bunch of fights, a lot of bad blood. So before we went down there, I said, 'They'd better have that ambulance full of gas.' After we dismantled them 44-0, I said, 'You know, I'm sorry, Everson Walls is right. Now we're 11-0, and we still ain't played anybody.'"

Ryan, who talked the talk and set the tone for the defense, had been on the Bears' staff since 1978. When Neill Armstrong was fired after the 1981 season, Gary Fencik and Alan Page circulated a petition among the defensive players to have Ryan retained. Halas agreed, but decided to hire Ditka as head coach. In so doing, he broke the unwritten rule that gives head coaches the authority to choose their own assistants. Add Ditka's and Ryan's volatile personalities into the mix and you had a shouting match waiting to happen.

"We basically had two head coaches," says Singletary. "That's why we carried them both off the field after the Super Bowl. They were so headstrong and stubborn. They were both cavalier, but they needed each other."

"Buddy did a great job," says Ditka. "At that time, he was as good a defensive coordinator as there was. But he wanted a head coaching job. When I got the job, it probably hurt him. Jim Finks was the GM at the time. He told me, 'I don't care what you do, but I want to keep the defensive coaches.' He said, 'You comfortable with that?' I said the only thing I wanted was an understanding that we weren't playing the Bears' defense, that we were in this together. That was the key to that season: We stayed together."

Not that it was easy. To the contrary. The nation got an up-close-and-personal look at the Ryan-Ditka relationship during the Bears' only loss of the season. It came on *NFL Monday Night Football* in Miami, where the Dolphins were hell-bent on preserving their 1972 team's legacy as the NFL's only unbeaten team. They won 38-24, thanks in part to Ryan's strategy, which called for a linebacker, Wilber Marshall, to cover wide receiver Nat Moore. With each passing touchdown, Ditka would rant and Ryan would rave.

"They didn't get along at all," says McMahon. "It was actually quite hilarious to watch them on the sideline. Once a week, somebody would make a big play on us. Every time, Ditka would yell 'We should play more zone!' And every time, Buddy would say, 'Leave me alone, this is my defense!' You've got to know Buddy. He doesn't care about anything but his defense. Never has, never will."

Ironically, McMahon got along better with Ryan than Ditka, whom McMahon would tweak at a moment's notice with his constant audibles. There were times when the Ditka-McMahon relationship was so strained, Ditka would call McMahon's agent, Steve Zucker, to act as a liaison. Not so with Ryan, who viewed McMahon as old school—headbands, sunglasses, and all.

"I always got along great with Buddy," says McMahon. "I think Buddy knew, as long as I was playing, we had a chance to win. I was going to do whatever it took, and he liked that. We would have scrimmages during summer camps, and the coordinators would pick the teams. Buddy would always pick me first, and the defensive players would say, 'Hey, what about me?' Buddy would say, 'Hey, I want to win the scrimmage.'"

With all those disparate personalities on the team, it took McMahon to bring the Bears together. He was so much more than the punk rocker in shoulder pads that the public knew. He was the Bobby Layne of his generation, a quarterback who, despite all the injuries, won 26 consecutive regular-season starts. His willingness to play in pain ingratiated him to Ryan and the veteran defensive players. He instilled a sense of purpose and a feeling of unity among his teammates that wasn't there before he arrived.

"He was the kind of guy who could get guys to rally around him," says Hampton. "We knew he was a little different when he showed up the day after they drafted him with a Budweiser in his hand. That wasn't surprising except it was nine-thirty in the morning. We had had other quarterbacks, but nobody ever took control of the position. By the end of his rookie year, we knew we could win with him. He wasn't a Dan Marino, a 6-5, 250-pound guy with a cannon, but the guy could play."

Says McMahon, "I think I had a big hand in turning us around as far as getting us to play as a team. Before, it was defense this, offense that. I got them to believe we couldn't win without each other. I used to go out with the offensive linemen at least once a week. By the end of the year, we'd have twenty or thirty guys showing up. Offense, defense, running backs, linemen...didn't matter."

During their week in New Orleans, the world was the Bears' stage. Bourbon Street was transformed into Rush Street South. The French Quarter became Danimal House. McMahon grew so weary of answering questions about his bruised buttocks, he mooned a helicopter hovering over the Bears' practice field. By Saturday night, the players were so restless, so anxious to meet their destiny, McMichael threw a metal chair at a chalkboard during the defense's final meeting. The chair hit with such force it wound up impaled in the middle of Ryan's Xs and Os.

"We knew Buddy was leaving to become the head coach in Philadelphia," says Fencik. "He told us that night, 'Win or lose, you'll always be my heroes.' I don't think there was a dry eye in the room. Then McMichael grabbed that chair and hurled it into the blackboard. You know what we did after that? We went on our milk-and-cookie break."

Champagne wasn't far behind. The Bears won 46-10 the next day in a game that ranked, at the time, as the most-lopsided Super Bowl ever. America couldn't get enough of the big lugs from the City of Big Shoulders. Super Bowl XX was seen by 127 million people across the country, surpassing the final episode of M*A*S*H as the most-watched television program in history.

Among all those viewers was Michael Jordan, who had suffered a broken foot early in his second NBA season. Jordan's time would have to wait. In January of 1986, in the aftermath of their season of seasons, it was Da Bears who owned Chicago and most points beyond. They were larger than life. Even larger than the Fridge.

"It was one of those moments you wish you could preserve forever," says Fencik. "It was like we were Paul Bunyan."

MICKEY HERSKOWITZ

WE HAVE MET THE ENEMY...

Sportswriters—the author included—
are hand fed everything they need at the
Super Bowl, and still they complain

FROM SUPER BOWL XXIV

FROM THE BEGINNING THERE WAS something weird going on with the Super Bowl. In time the problem became clear. It was us: the media. Never have so many complained so loudly about so much pampering.

It is a quirky quality, but one we can't seem to shake. No matter how much we get fed, entertained, and weighed down with souvenirs and press releases, we grump about how shamelessly the Super Bowl is "hyped." We do this with the splendid and innocent detachment of politicians crying out against big government.

More than any event, the Super Bowl is a writer's game. It is, in fact, a writer's week. We are provided with everything but an opening paragraph and a pillow for a halftime nap. And we reply with endless bellyaching about being manipulated, about being bused to press interviews, about being forced to consume great quantities of Gulf shrimp and lobster claws.

It is time that someone had the class to acknowledge that this is so and say that our conduct has been shabby. Still, we are what we are. The typical sportswriter would complain about the scent of the soap in the restrooms aboard Malcolm Forbes' yacht.

Fishing through an old collection of notes, I ran across this paragraph: "Once the hype is over, once the blimp is in the air, the fans are in their seats and the buildup is over, it will be what a Super Bowl ought to be: a football game."

It no longer matters who wrote the words or in what paper they appeared. I might have written them myself. One way or another, we all have. But after 24 of them (and this year's game makes 23 for me), I ask myself: a football game? That's it? Jeez, what a letdown. With a media army of 2,000 on hand, we at least could stage the invasion of Grenada.

Of course, there *are* no wars the week of the Super Bowl. You can look it up. The generals and the admirals don't have the time. Like everyone else, they are too busy reading about the game, wading through miles of newspaper copy, interviews with players, coaches, wives, hotel clerks, and cab drivers. Writers even interview other writers. We are everywhere, hovering like fruit flies, swarming across the fields and the locker rooms, digging, always digging, for an angle, a quote, a fact, a crumb.

One year Milton Richman of *United Press International* visited a Louisiana leper colony to get the residents' reaction to the Super Bowl in nearby New Orleans. In the category of reaching for a fresh angle, Milt has a special place in our hearts.

Of course, it has become one of the great cliches of sports journalism that the drama is not always on the field. The press has done its best to turn the Super Bowl into a self-fulfilling prophecy. Here are a few of our favorite examples:

• There was the night before Super Bowl VIII when a Houston vice squad burst into press headquarters and busted a writers' poker game. No one was booked, but the words of Chicago's Rick Talley still ring as clearly as freedom's bell: "NO ONE MOVES UNTIL WE FINISH THIS HAND."

• Jim Schaaf of the Kansas City Chiefs made it into the Public Relations Hall of Fame with his reaction under fire the night the Len Dawson gambling story broke the week of Super Bowl IV. When two writers arrived early at the Chiefs' official hotel suite, Schaaf asked, "Will there be a lot more writers arriving?"

"I'm afraid there will, Jimmy," said one of the writers.

Schaaf picked up the phone and said, "Hello, room service? Send up five pounds of shrimp remoulade."

• If one scene endures as a symbol of what this event has meant to sports literature, it would have to be Duane Thomas, of Dallas, throwing Super Bowl VI into confusion by the inspired process of saying nothing. A near panic developed one day when Thomas, who was sitting in the practice field bleachers, moved his lips. Writers rushed up, breathlessly, from everywhere. "What happened?" one of them asked.

"He moved his lips," was the answer.

"When they moved, what did they say?"

"They said, 'I don't feel like talking.'"

• Even hardened newsmen were touched when Lou Michaels, the kicker for the Baltimore Colts, talked about facing his brother Walt, then the defensive coach of the Jets in Super Bowl III. He talked about their home in Swoyersville, Pennsylvania, their early life, how they depended on each other. He was crying. He didn't want the writers to leave. Later, Paul Zimmerman, then with the *New York Post*, said to Jimmy Orr, the Colts' receiver: "Gee, did you see the way Lou Michaels was crying during that press interview?"

Orr nodded. "If you were out drinking vodka till 6 A.M.," he said, "and there was a stiff wind blowing across your face, you'd be crying, too."

• The media had a field day when the Tampa City Council passed a resolution "adopting" the Redskins before their date with the Raiders, a team then located somewhere between Oakland and Los Angeles. When the charter flight carrying the Raiders to Super Bowl XVIII landed, a local hostess began apologizing to the players. "It doesn't matter," one of them said. "We're not welcome anywhere."

TONY HILLERMAN

WHEN QUARTERBACKS DIDN'T WEAR SKIRTS

Novelist Tony Hillerman remembers a time
when football was a simpler game—but that
doesn't mean it was better then

FROM SUPER BOWL XXX

I WONDER HOW MANY PEOPLE at Super Bowl XXX remember the days when a quarterback throwing an interception faced a real risk of paying for his carelessness by playing a couple of downs as a defensive back. I'd guess about 10 percent, and they'll be crusty old senior citizens such as me who also remember nickel hamburgers and rumble seats.

As I recall (and those of us who remember nickel hamburgers don't always have reliable recollections), the rules in those days provided that a coach could substitute no more than four players when possession of the ball changed. Or maybe it was two after each down. Whatever it was, I loved it. It offered defensive linemen such as me a chance for revenge.

As every football fan knows, offensive blockers have an unfair advantage over defenders. They know the snap count, where the running back is supposed to be going, and so forth. But that old limited substitution rule gave us defenders our chance to do some paying back for at least a down or two.

My team, the Konawa (Oklahoma) High School Tigers, ran a Single Wing offense, as did just about every other high school in America in those days. When the first stringer was hurt or tired, I played middle guard on defense. That meant that when the Bowlegs Drillers, or the Maud Mavericks, or the Wetumka Buffalos, or the Tecumseh Braves, or the Pearson Switch Pintos, ran one of those off-tackle plays, the strongside offensive guard in front of me would block the tackle and let me charge through the hole. Whereupon I would be blindsided by the enemy's weakside pulling guard. Guard trap, I think it's called. (And, by the way, those were the actual names of the schools competing for class C honors in our district of Oklahoma.)

Whether you call it a guard trap or not, that was its effect, and it inflicted bruises, sore ribs, and humiliation upon the defender. It was designed to neutralize linemen such as me, who compensated for a lack of what is now called "athleticism" with a sort of fierce damn-the-torpedoes enthusiasm for crashing into running backs. That made us slow to learn. It tended to be somewhere in the third quarter—after a halftime chewing-out by the coach—before we had begun understanding what was happening to us and had begun to take countermeasures.

The bright side of this situation was being left in after our side got the ball. Because the coach wanted to replace defensive backs with guys better schooled in ball handling, and because he could make only four substitutions, we linemen got to stay in for a play or two and often more, because little schools such as ours didn't have a wealth of replacements.

That made me the weakside guard on offense, the pulling guard, the guy who got to be the executioner on the guard trap. In other words, JOY! I got to clobber the same guy who had been doing it to me all day.

In my case, the situation even allowed me to become a ball carrier on one glorious occasion. I still remember the thrill of that. I suspect Coach does, too. It caused him to be reprimanded by the school board.

Then as now in Oklahoma, football is king, and at Konawa every physically able boy tried out for the team. That gave the coach a pool of about 30 kids from which to pick, and, despite the small number, a wide range of abilities. That was because in those days no one had imposed an age ceiling.

Konawa High was a mixed school, the student body including about one-third "oil patch" kids, who were bused in from the wherever the drilling rigs were working in the Seminole and Earlsboro oil fields. Another third, of which I was a member, were farmers' kids bused in from the cotton patches and corn fields. Another third were town kids.

Our better players tended to be fellows who went to school episodically, dropping out when jobs as "roughnecks" or "swampers" were available on the drilling rigs. Thus our ace fullback was 25 years old, and the center and tackle I played between when I was a 15-year-old junior both were at least 20.

Other schools in our class C league had about the same situation—except for Bowlegs, which was purely an oil-boom town. And it was at Bowlegs where I got my only chance to carry the ball.

I once overheard Coach remarking, "Hillerman is little, but he's slow." On this day, I was slower than usual.

The play in question was the Konawa Tigers' version of the off-tackle plunge. I was supposed to pull out, run behind the center, and deal with any defender who might have broken through. If none had, I was supposed to lead interference through the hole made by the strongside tackle.

This Saturday afternoon I was a wee bit late, reaching the hole behind the fullback instead of ahead of him. This caused him to be leading interference for me. The linebacker I was assigned to block slammed him with such gusto that the football flew backward, striking me on the chest. I clutched it, charged forward at least 2 yards, and was thereupon demolished so thoroughly by a swarm of defenders that it became one of those rare double-fumble plays.

Coach was fairly tolerant for a man of his profession, and his re-action to this would not have gotten him into trouble had Bowlegs had the sort of facilities available to high schools today. But the Bowlegs gridiron was a grassless expanse, graded flat by an oil company's bulldozer. The yard markers were rolled on with some white material which I like to believe was chalk but might have been quicklime. (It's cheaper, and environmental hazard laws were not imposed in those days.) But what did in Coach was the absence of bleachers.

At Bowlegs, fans lined the playing field with their pickup trucks. They watched the game perched on bumpers, fenders, tailgates, and hoods, celebrating their team's successes with a symphony of horn honking.

This arrangement gave fans an intimate view of the action (one of our wide receivers once ran over his mother when he was driv-en out of bounds). Alas, it also put people in position to hear what was said on the bench, and this was what caused Coach his prob-lem.

My tardy arrival at the hole had so provoked Coach that he did-n't notice that Bowlegs supporters had stopped serenading their team's fumble recovery. The Konawa moms and dads just behind him heard what he was shouting to me even more clearly than I did and were more affected by it because I had heard it often in previous games.

"Hillerman," he bellowed, "you run like a [expletive deleted] dog!" I have replaced Coach's colorful language in deference to NFL fans who might be offended—as were the parents who protested Coach's language to the school board at its next meeting.

Suffice it to say that Coach had compared my running to that of a male dog whose reproductive ability had been impaired by in-jury. This may surprise younger fans conditioned to contemporary trash talk but those were gentler times. Our idea of ribald was to state that "the only way to get to Maud is through Bowlegs." A look at an Oklahoma road map (if Bowlegs hasn't faded away with the oil boom) shows that to be true, but in those days it was not said in mixed company.

Shortly after my moment of glory as a ball carrier, Pearl Harbor was bombed, the 45th National Guard Division was mobilized, including our entire backfield and most of the rest of us, and the Konawa Tigers became the Willie and Joe of Bill Mauldin's famous World War II cartoons.

In the postwar world, the days of limited substitution were numbered, soon to be replaced by two-platoon football with its swarm of coaches, specialty teams, Nickel backs, skill positions, rules against putting dents in quarterbacks, and so forth. It happened first in college ball (or maybe the pros started it) and spread like dandelions through the ranks of the nation's high schools.

I saw part of that tragedy unfold from the press seats while covering football for the old and lamented *United Press*. One year we were watching All-America halfbacks looking silly at safety, and quarterbacks trying to outsmart each other on pass patterns, and the next it was all over.

There was no more getting even in this new world. The line clearly was drawn between defenders and offenders. One no longer did both jobs. Before long, defensive teams began looking at teammates on the offensive side as well-muscled sissies.

I think it was Jack Lambert, the great middle linebacker for the Pittsburgh Steelers' Steel Curtain defense, who said it first: "Quarterbacks should wear skirts." By then the sentiment had become common on the blue-collar side of the line.

But loss of the revenge factor wasn't the only price paid with the change to unlimited substitutions. Some of the great schools in the game dropped out, or dropped into virtually obscure categories. The list is long, a litany of the great colleges of my boyhood: Carnegie Tech, the University of Chicago, Loyola, Fordham with its "Seven Blocks of Granite" line, Villanova, Holy Cross, and Creighton, and all those Ivy League teams that now play out of the spotlight.

The first time I saw a team beat the Oklahoma Sooners—already on their way to their unprecedented string of national championships—it was Santa Clara. But the death of the limited substitution rule was also the death of Santa Clara football and of that sort of David-beating-Goliath business.

The Davids of the NCAA world can't afford to hire two platoons of coaches, or to redshirt a dorm full of big, fast players to keep them from signing with the competition.

Ah, well, not all the changes affecting football since my days as a second-stringer for the Konawa Tigers were bad. Our mixture of farm kids, town boys, and oil patchers also was a mix of white and Indians. The Indians in turn were a mix of Seminoles, Potawatomies, and Black Foot.

Our best halfback was a Seminole. One day he was missing from the seat ahead of me in English class, and at football practice. And to make the story short, he never returned to Konawa High. No one ever told us what happened, but we found out.

As was the case in much of the South in those days, an Oklahoma law prohibited blacks and whites from attending the same schools. Someone had filed formal notice with the school board claiming that there was a black ancestor somewhere in the family tree of our Seminole halfback.

Segregation, they called it. It made our halfback's presence in that chair ahead of me in English and on the football team a crime.

He was supposed to be enrolled in a "separate but equal" black school. But there was no black high school anywhere near Konawa. I never found out what happened to him. But when I remember that incident, it makes me downright delighted with the changes I see from football, circa 1941, to football, 1996.

HI, MY NAME IS DAVE

What does a comedian know about football? He knows you can't score without a good punch line

FROM SUPER BOWL XXIX

"YOU HAVE TO FEEL SORRY for the Bills. Four straight Super Bowls they've lost. Although this year, they will receive the home version of the Super Bowl and a year's supply of Turtle Wax."

"The Bills have a new slogan: We're never going to Disney World."

"Here's something I didn't know: When CBS was outbid by FOX for the rights to the National Football Conference, the third-highest bid was from Madonna."

"New York Giants quarterback Dave Brown appeared at a public school in the Bronx and gave a phys-ed lesson to 125 fourth-graders. The good news is, he was sacked only three times."

"Here's a travel advisory: The Buffalo, New York, airport is closed—not because of weather. It's just that the Buffalo people don't want the Bills to come back."

"The New York Giants lost [again] this weekend. To give you an idea how bad it's getting, in the fourth quarter, 50,000 fans at Giants Stadium started chanting, 'Let's Go Mets.'"

"When the FOX network outbid CBS by more than $100 million for the rights to broadcast NFL games, CBS officials admitted they didn't have the money to match FOX's bid. Great, so now it's my fault."

"I get a call just before we're ready to get on the air and it's my mother back in Indiana. I pick up the phone and say, 'Mom, what is it, is there a problem?' And she says, 'Well, I don't know. Did you tape the Super Bowl for me?'"

And Now, for Tonight's Top 10 Lists...
FROM THE HOME OFFICE IN SIOUX CITY, IOWA...
Top 10 Ways to Make the Super Bowl Even More Exciting
10. Replace Gatorade with Nyquil.
9. Residents of winning city don't have to pay taxes for a year.
8. For final quarter, coat field with nacho cheese stuff.
7. Super Glue ball to quarterback's hand; sit back and watch the fun.
6. 11 players, 10 uniforms.
5. Fill the ball with angry, stinging hornets.
4. If you go offsides, you have to kiss Dan Dierdorf on the lips.
3. New position: mailman with a rifle.
2. Complete a pass, do a shot.
And the number-one way to make the Super Bowl even more exciting:
    Blimp fights.

Top 10 Signs Your Team Won't Be Going to the Super Bowl

10. Last year's mascot is this year's quarterback.
9. Players beaten by local teens in halftime Punt, Pass & Kick competition.
8. Inner-ear condition makes it impossible for starting halfback to stay between sidelines.
7. Just to be on the safe side, they often punt on first down.
6. They're constantly taking time outs to consult with Robert Shapiro.
5. More players on smoking side of bench than non-smoking.
4. Whenever they manage to get a first down, they dump a bucket of Gatorade over the head coach.
3. Players constantly addressing each other as "girlfriend."
2. Starting fullback: Richard Simmons.

And the number-one sign your team won't be going to the Super Bowl:
   Instead of helmets, turbans.

Top 10 Things Marv Levy Said at Halftime of Super Bowl XXVIII

10. "We won! Woo! We're Super Bowl champs!"
9. "Boy, I'm sleepy. You guys sleepy?"
8. "We've got a long trip home after the game, so I don't want anyone wearing themselves out."
7. "Now get out there and rest on your laurels."
6. "Hey, Kelly, leave some champagne for everyone else."
5. "What do you mean there are two more quarters?"
4. "Let's plan exactly how you're gonna dump the Gatorade on me."
3. "Okay, boys—get out there and start sucking."
2. "Wait a minute. If we win, we have to go to Disney World."

And the number-one thing Marv Levy said at halftime of Super Bowl XXVIII:
   "Hey fellas, more fudge?"

CARL HIAASEN

LAMENT OF A DOLFAN

The best-selling author of Striptease
couldn't bear to watch his favorite team...
but couldn't bear to look the other way

FROM SUPER BOWL XXIX

I T'S LATE SEPTEMBER, when most NFL quarterbacks still are
ambulatory, and most teams still own at least a mathematical
shot at the Super Bowl.

Among the perennial contenders are the Miami Dolphins, my
hometown team. By the time you read this column, we'll know if
the Fins are making their sixth trip to the big game.

What a thrill that would be!

Unfortunately, it's a thrill that some of us won't be able to share.
If the Dolphins are going to the Super Bowl, I'm not. I don't dare
attend, or watch it on television, or even listen on radio. Not if I
want them to win.

Weird, but true: Whenever I pay attention to a Dolphins game,
bad things happen. Spooky, creepy, otherwordly occurrences:
unprovoked fumbles, phantom penalties, season-ending injuries,

forward laterals, bobbled snaps—you name it.

For that reason, I practice abstinence through absence—total sensory deprivation—on game day.

The only time I saw a game at Joe Robbie Stadium, the Dolphins suffered a transcendental second-half collapse against the Buffalo Bills. I bolted in the third quarter—too late to help. Staying home is safer, with abundant distractions to keep one's mind off football.

I've deliberately chosen to write this column while the Dolphins are playing the Minnesota Vikings in Minneapolis. It's on TV right this minute. Fortunately, I've got this important magazine assignment to hold my attention.

Otherwise, I'd be tempted to peek at the game, at which point misfortune would flatten the Dolphins like a Mack truck.

You don't believe it? Let's try a little test. Okay, I'm getting up. I'm walking to the living room. I'm turning on the television...

...and there's Vikings running back Terry Allen, barreling into the end zone for a touchdown. Fourteen-zip and it's only the first quarter.

I rest my case.

Creeping back to the keyboard, I resume typing....

Quirky superstitions are a colorful tradition of professional sports. Every golfer has a lucky putter. Every baseball hitter has a lucky bat. Every hockey player has a lucky cup.

Maybe every NFL franchise has an unlucky fan, some karma-deficient soul who hexes the team merely by rooting for it. Maybe my equivalent in Tampa seldom misses a game.

In the case of my own ruinous effect on the Dolphins, the paranormal pattern began to emerge after 1972, when Miami had the only perfect season in NFL history.

Seventeen victories, zero defeats.

Try to imagine what that meant to glory-starved fans of an expansion team that began in 1966. Many of us who were born in Florida grew up with the weekly agonies of the fledgling franchise. To this day, we have recurring nightmares in which the Dolphins' first coach, George Wilson Sr., installs his own son, George Wilson Jr., as quarterback! Bizarre as it seems, this actually happened.

In those early days, every Dolphins' victory was either a gift from God or a freak accident. To ascend so quickly from the pit of the sport to the pinnacle—a perfect season—was a supernatural achievement.

And I'm afraid it ruined us.

(Do I dare check the game against the Vikings?)

...and there's Terry Kirby, the Dolphins' shifty young running back, getting stuffed on an attempted two-point conversion. Not merely stuffed, but pretzeled.

Now he's being hauled off the field in a flatbed cart. Out for the year! This is terrible, and it's all my fault. I mean, there's a perfectly riveting bass-fishing show on cable—why couldn't I watch that?

Halftime score: A 28-6 drubbing, with Miami being the drubee.

Off goes the tube.

After an undefeated season, it's inevitable that a team's fortunes will go downhill, statistically and spiritually.

But the Dolphins immediately won a second Super Bowl. The year after that, they stayed on top of the AFC East. Although star players such as Larry Csonka, Jim Kiick, and Paul Warfield departed the next year for the short-lived comedic enterprise called the World Football League, the Dolphins still were a very good team.

They did, however, lose now and then. Grumbling—and the occasional snide murmur—was heard from the stands.

During the late 1970s, Miami experienced a few average season—seasons that would have buoyed sports fans in, say, Cincinnati or New England. But "average" doesn't cut it here. Spoiled by perfection, many Dolphins boosters found losing intolerable, and devoted Sundays to improving their tans.

It was during that trying post-Csonka era that my brother and I, independently of one another, began bolting from our TVs at the first hint of trouble in the game. Sometimes we fled in dread, sometimes in disgust, sometimes in despair.

But flee we did. It was undeniably gutless and sniveling behavior, but the alternative was to hurl a can of beer nuts through the television screen. Running from the house seemed more mature.

Interestingly, my brother and I both noticed—again, independently—that the Dolphins invariable sparked to life as soon as we quit watching. If we peeked at the tube, we'd find that our beloved Fins suddenly had acquired a running game or a pass defense, and were rallying in miraculous fashion.

(A masochistic time out, for a check of events in the Metrodome...)

...It's the third quarter. The DOLPHINS are down 28-14. Minnesota just missed a field goal, and now Miami is driving. Keith Byars runs for good yardage off right tackle! Marino hits O.J. McDuffie on a curl!

Then Marino passes to—a man in the wrong-colored uniform. A Vikings linebacker, it would seem.

Off goes the TV!

During the not-so-super years, many fair-weather fans abandoned the Dolphins. Then the team drafted a quarterback from the University of Pittsburgh named Dan Marino. We'd never seen anything like him. Nobody had.

Suddenly it became a test not to watch the games, even if watching wasn't in the best interest of the team. A radiant talent such as Marino appears maybe once in a fan's life—and a very lucky fan, at that. So my brother and I both caved in, tentatively returning to the fold on Sunday afternoons.

True sports nuts understand: A star player gives you something to cheer for, even in the absence of a star team.

When I attended college in Atlanta, occasionally I would go downtown to watch a baseball game. This was back when the Braves stunk to high heaven, but it didn't matter because they had an outfielder named Henry Aaron. In those years, waiting for Aaron to hit home runs was the only reason any sane human would sit through nine innings of Braves baseball.

For football fans in Florida, Dan Marino has the same magnetism. He's always been a joy to see, even when the team founders.

The Dolphins of the mid-1980s didn't stink to high heaven. Relative to most franchises, they didn't stink at all. Thanks to Marino's platinum arm, they made it to Super Bowl XIX against the 49ers.

(Speaking of which, the festivities in Minneapolis ought to be winding down...)

...Ah ha! What'd I tell you?

While I was busy writing, the Dolphins heroically bounced back from a 28-point deficit to tie the game! Now they're trailing 35-28 in the fourth quarter, with loads of time left on the clock.

But as soon as I plant my butt in front of the television, Miami begins to falter. The Dolphins' secondary appears to have gotten hold of some bad Gatorade, judging by the wooziness with which it now blows the most elementary pass coverages. Vikings quarterback Warren Moon and his receivers are having a splendid time.

Off goes the tube!

In chatting with other NFL fans, I've discovered the video abstinence, though unpublicized, is more widely practiced than experts believe.

Deprivation therapy is especially common in cities in which the football team has wallowed for years with no realistic expectation of reaching the Super Bowl. Some fans have suffered so long that avoiding the games is a medical necessity to stave off depression and gastrointestinal afflictions.

I creep back to the TV for the end of the Miami-Minnesota shootout...

...It's 38-35, with one minute to go. The Dolphins are trailing, but they just scored. Marino already has thrown for 3 touchdowns, a few of which I hope to see on the postgame highlights show.

Now comes the onside kick. Customarily this is when I'd dash outside to do some emergency weeding, but this afternoon I'm glued to the tube, for the sake of the experiment.

Stoyanovich carefully places the ball on the tee, steps back, raises his hand. There's the kickoff, hopping, squibbing, tumbling....

And there are the Vikings, snatching it out of the air and falling securely to the ground. Game's over.

Enervated by guilt, I slump on the sofa as the final seconds tick off the clock. Damn. I shouldn't have given in.

Later, out of scientific curiosity, I phone my brother in Baltimore. As I suspected, he'd succumbed to the same urge: He'd watched the game, too. We are a weak-willed clan.

Forgive us, Dan. I wish I could promise it won't happen again.

JAMES W. HALL

RELUCTANT ZEALOT

The author concedes that he is an ardent,
adamant, involved fan—but that's not the
same as a football nerd

FROM SUPER BOWL XXIX

I T'S A PERFECT NOVEMBER AFTERNOON in south Florida. A cool front has moved through overnight and scraped the sky clean. It is now an immaculate, cerulean blue, the color of Paul Newman's eyes or the pool water at the Coral Gables Country Club. A lazy cinnamon scented breeze is stirring the palm fronds and there seems to be more air in this new air. Overnight, our old stagnant, humid atmosphere has been washed away, replaced by this new stuff straight from Canada with its hint of pine and glaciers, as invigorating as a jolt of Cuban coffee.

My fishing boat is filled with gas. The Yamaha is tuned and greased, the deck is washed. My reels are lubed, filled with fresh line. There is word among my fisherman buddies that dolphin are showing up in great numbers very close to shore. The backcountry waters are full of bonefish and tarpon. Everywhere there are fish jumping into boats. The seas are as flat as putting greens.

But on this beautiful, inviting afternoon, I'm locked away inside the house, making the guacamole, tearing open the Cheese Doodles, foaming up my first beer. Because today is Game Day. The only Dolphins I care about on this sunny afternoon are putting on their shoulder pads, getting ready to play at Joe Robbie Stadium.

I could have gone to the game. A friend invited me, but for the hundredth time I declined. I love football, but I don't like crowds. Well, that's not entirely true. I just don't like being in crowds. The fact is, I like crowds very much when I'm looking at them on TV. I like hearing them roar, I like The Wave, I like the white hankies. Without fans filling the stands, my afternoons in front of the television wouldn't be half as much fun.

I'm glad there are those who enjoy being in crowds. They are a necessary ingredient in my pleasure. I like their wacky signs, outrageous puns and plays on the call letters of the network televising the game. I like the ones who paint their faces in team colors, the ones with the crazy hats. I like the ones who go half-naked in the middle of winter in Buffalo. Though, as a Miami fan there is little else I can allow myself to like about Buffalo or its fans.

I like the fans who sit on the 50-yard line and watch most of the game on their portable TVs. And though you are not supposed to say so, I like the pretty women fans. It pleases me that there are several cameramen who constantly roam the stands looking for shots of them. So what if it is politically incorrect to admit? This is Sunday. This is Game Day. The one day of the week when political correctness and correctness of every kind take a holiday.

But let's be clear about this: I am not a football nerd. I never have memorized a single statistic about football. I have only a dim memory of who won the Super Bowl V or X years ago, though I'm sure I watched those games. I don't know the names of any of the Dolphins' assistant coaches, or any of the special-teams players. This is a crucial distinction for us understated football fans—not to be mistaken for football nerds. In this case, I am much like those drivers on the interstates of America who believe that anyone driving 10 miles faster or 10 miles slower than they're driving has to be a complete lunatic.

I mention to my neighbor that I am going to be watching the Big Game today and he looks at me blankly. What Big Game? And I see him staring at me the same way I stare at the geeks who can name the first 500 college players who will be selected in this year's NFL draft or the 40-yard dash time for some halfback at Alcorn State. I am not that kind of geek. I am the Cheese Doodle, a quiet fan geek.

We are the fans who have otherwise productive lives. Yes, we read the sports page, listen to an occasional sports talk show, make sure the guacamole is ready for the pregame show. We give up glorious Sunday afternoons to lie on the couch in front of the 32-inch. But, by God, we absolutely and utterly refuse to memorize statistics. And, more importantly, we are the fans who have made conscious and deeply emotional decisions to stick with our team through thick and thin.

This is a pivotal distinction between us and other fans. My loyalty to the Miami Dolphins is frail and vacillating. For more than 20 years I have worked hard to discover ways to disentangle myself from an emotional connection to the weekly fate of the Dolphins. Being a sensible, reasonable adult, I sometimes manage to talk myself out of it. The conversation goes like this: Whether the Fish win or lose on Sunday obviously should have no connection with my sense of worth, my emotional inner landscape. If Dan Marino has a cold afternoon, or if the Fins once again produce less than a hundred yards on the ground, or if the defense again finds no way to stop the 10-yard down-and-out, why should I be depressed? Why should I writhe on the couch sinking deeper into the hollow gloom of defeat? Why should I wake up Monday morning feeling a sense of failure? There is utterly no good reason for it. Such feelings surely are deeply neurotic weaknesses, some undiscovered form of dependency that not even the Betty Ford Clinic people have tackled yet.

However, when this first line of defense fails, as it frequently does, I must resort to a more devious approach—to watch the game with a predetermined sense of doom. These guys'll be lucky to lose by only 2 touchdowns. I'll just sit here and concentrate on how bad the running game is this week. Cheese Doodles at the ready, I will razz and snort, mock and rant. See, I knew it! These guys are worthless teases. They get so close, then they unfailingly disappoint.

The obvious danger with such a strategy is that I might actually begin to believe these things and become so cynical that I stop watching altogether. This almost happened three or four years ago, but the anxiety and withdrawal were so painful that I had to revert to my earlier methods and give myself a good talking to—your fate is not tied to these guys, don't get so worked up. Miss a few weekends, dry out, see how you feel.

Another technique I have been refining lately relies on the special identity that my team has established over the Don Shula era. These guys are notoriously clean players. Season after season they are the least penalized team in the league. Therefore, my rationalizing logic goes, they are so under control, so gentlemanly and fair-minded that it is to their credit even to play close with their bad, brawling, morally inferior opponents. I tell myself that I prefer the Dolphins to play the righteous game they do instead of the smash-mouth football that seems to be the rage these days, even if it means my guys will most likely lose the big ones.

Or I might use a permutation of this team-specific approach: Shula is the winningest coach of all time, and Dan Marino is among the top two or three greatest quarterbacks. And don't forget the 1972 perfect season. I can console and distract myself endlessly with these facts, no matter how poorly they may be playing on a given afternoon. Sure, the glorification of winning is a sad and empty thing. Clearly, this team has virtues far beyond its won-lost record, and surely it is worth giving up my sunny Sunday afternoons to watch them, no matter what the outcome.

Complicating matters with this approach, however, is the fact that I am also a reluctant Miami Hurricane fan. A deft and malleable psychological yoga is required to allow me to root for the cleanest team in professional football with the same enthusiasm as I cheer on college football's nose-thumbing rowdy boys.

Somehow I've managed. I have screamed at the television on more beautiful Miami afternoons than is good for anyone. I have scared the dog, frightened my spouse. I have consumed foods of grotesquely unnatural colors, foods I would never dream of eating at any other time. And though we at-home fans clearly don't have the crass and obvious effect of fans in the stands, drowning out the play calling of the opposition, and pumping up our brave gladiators, nevertheless, I am convinced we are a crucial, if unseen, ingredient in our team's success.

Despite having no scientific proof whatsoever, I have come to believe that fans like me radiate a crucial network of psychic energy. In some pivotal way, it is our couch-twisting that gets Keith Jackson that extra yard for the first down, our fist-shaking, name-calling cheers and gasps that give the extra push that propels the game-winning field goal through the uprights. I am as certain of this as I am that I have helped, in my way, to steer the Dolphins down the field with powerful discharges of hope and dread.

Finally, I have come to believe that this weekly struggle to maintain a balance between loyalty to my team and common sense has much in common with the natural ebb and flow of an enduring marriage. The Dolphins and I are locked into a fierce and passionate intertwining of destinies. And all these spats, this continually strained fidelity, these rationalizing gymnastics I must inflict upon myself, all these are probably nothing more than the natural transactions of a long and thriving romance.

JOHN WIEBUSCH

IT DOESN'T GET
ANY BETTER

*No matter how many times you
have been to the Super Bowl, you keep
getting caught up in its magic*

FROM SUPER BOWL XXIX

THE SUPER BOWL THAT will be played in Joe Robbie Stadium today will be my XXVth. My last wedding anniversary also was my XXVth, but that's another story.

After all those years, after all those ultimate big-game experiences, you might think that I would be a little cynical, You might think that maybe I might even be taking it all for granted.

Fat chance.

Fact is, this is the Super Bowl. *The Super Bowl.* And there is nothing like it—nothing in American culture. It's not just the game I am talking about, it's the *Event.* Tbe World Series comes closest. But compared to the Super Bowl, the World Series is *Star Search* alongside a great Broadway musical.

The danger, of course, for the several thousand people lucky enough to be here each year is that the game almost becomes an anticlimax. After a week of media scrutiny, of nonstop socializing, of lavish and memorable parties (I know people whose reference to past Super Bowls is the Friday night Commissioner's Party, as it has come to be known, or the Tailgate Party at the stadium the day of the game)...well, after all that you sometimes have to remind yourself there's still a *game* to be played.

For me, the games are eternally memorable, even when the final score sounds like the Christians against the lions in ancient Rome.

If you had been in the Superdome for the Patriots against the Bears in Super Bowl XX, I guarantee that you never would forget the powerful energy of the Chicago fans and their team of destiny. I guarantee that you would never forget the playing of the Bears' video, "The Super Bowl Shuffle," on the stadium message board at halftime. Richter could have measured the tremor in the Superdome. And the cheer when the video ended? Who cares that the final score was 46-10?

The same is true of Super Bowl XXII in San Diego in which the final score was 42-10. What I'll never forget is Washington quarterback Doug Williams triggering the most thrilling 15 minutes of one-team action I've ever seen. With Williams passing for 4 touchdowns and 228 yards, the Redskins scored 35 points against Denver in about the time it takes to shave and shower.

The big-game effect is cumulative. I think of the cocky pre- and postgame swaggers of the people from Pittsburgh, Dallas, and San Francisco. And the sad faces from Minnesota, Denver, and Buffalo.

Super Bowl events are mountain streams of memories for me. There is not enough room here for me to tell you about all of them.

Ask me to name the most memorable of the 25 games, and I would select my first one, Super Bowl V, in Miami.

I was there to go to the game, of course. But mostly I was there to do interviews for a book I was putting together on the life of Vince Lombardi, who had died of cancer four months before.

I stayed at the Fontainebleau Hotel, ironically the same hotel I stayed at this year (in 1971, the Fontainebleau was a wilted flower; in 1995, the Fontainebleau has its petals open again, like most of renovated Miami Beach).

In 1971, the Fontainebleau was next door to the Kennilworth Hotel. Fifteen or so years later, they put explosives under the Kermilworth and brought it down in one swoop. But in 1971, the Kennilworth still had glamour, still had not lost its figure.

You will know that was true when I tell you that it was the hotel where NFL owners and executives were staying. NFL owners and officials never stay at places where they leave the light on.

I arrived in Miami on the Monday before the game, and I went over to the Kennilworth to find my friend Jim Finks, the Vikings' general manager and a pal from my journalistic days in Minneapolis. Finks took me around to the cabanas of NFL owners.

"This punk kid doesn't look old enough to buy a beer," Finks said to George Halas, "but he's doing a book on Vince...and he's all right."

I spent two hours with Halas talking about his legendary Green Bay rival. After that, Papa Bear was my friend until the day he died at age 88 in 1983.

Finks introduced me to Pete Rozelle and Jim Kensil, to Wellington Mara and Art Modell, to Art Rooney and Dan Rooney, to Tex Schramm and Edward Bennett Williams, to Dan Reeves (the Rams' owner) and Lou Spadia. Only Mara, Modell, and Dan Rooney still are involved with the game today (Jim Finks has joined Lombardi, Halas, Art Rooney, Reeves, and Williams in that Higher League).

I floated home with four notebooks of scribblings and a dozen tapes.

Oh, yes, there was a game that year, too. In a contest dubbed the Blunder Bowl, there were a total of 11 turnovers. Not exactly beautiful? Yes. Anything but exciting? Hardly. Who could forget Jim O'Brien's tie-breaking field goal in the final seconds? Who could forget the Cowboys' Bob Lilly throwing his helmet 60 yards in disgust over the Baltimore Colts' 16-13 victory?

So I test myself by saying: *The Super Bowl is only a game. The Super Bowl is only a game. The Super Bowl is only a game.*

Yeah. And Cindy Crawford is only a woman.

RAY DIDINGER

THE MILD SIDE OF BROADWAY

One lifestyle change and many years
later, the legend of quarterback
Joe Namath remains alive and well

FROM SUPER BOWL XXVIII

D AVE HERMAN RECALLS the summer of 1968 when the New York Jets and Green Bay Packers were in Cleveland for a preseason doubleheader.

The two teams stayed at the same hotel, and before the games (Jets vs. Detroit and the Packers vs. Cleveland) the lobby was jammed with autograph seekers. But these were not your typical kids with NFL lunch boxes.

"Most of them were girls, all dolled up like they were waiting for a Hollywood producer," says Herman, a guard with the Jets. "When Joe Namath stepped off the elevator, it was like a stampede. People went crazy, screaming, climbing over each other just to touch him.

"Five minutes later, Bart Starr walked through the same lobby and nobody looked twice. That's when I realized what the word charisma means. Starr was a great quarterback, but Namath was that and more. Joe was a true superstar, maybe the greatest ever."

Joe Namath. Broadway Joe.

In the tumultuous America of the late 1960s, the Jets' swaggering young quarterback was the cover boy of professional football. He was talented, he was brash, he was glamorous. Whether he was passing for 496 yards in a game (which he did) or throwing 6 interceptions (he did that, too), he had fans lined up at the stage door.

He guaranteed a victory over Baltimore in Super Bowl III, and he delivered with an MVP performance as the Jets shocked the Colts 16-7. It was the first meaningful win for the upstart American Football League against the established National Football League, and it validated the merger of the two, which was agreed upon in 1966 and fully enacted in 1970.

Today, when people talk about the Super Bowl, they often bypass Vince Lombardi, whose Green Bay Packers won the first two games of the series, and start with Namath and the Jets. More than any other man, Broadway Joe married the game and the spectacle. He put the Super Bowl at the top of the American sports marquee.

In October, 1969, *Esquire* magazine wrote: "Once in a generation, more or less, a chosen figure detaches himself from the social matrix and swims into mythology, hovering somewhere near the center of the universe, organizing in himself our attention, monopolizing our hopes and fears, compelling our hearts to beat as his.

"Such a figure is Joe Namath."

Twenty-five years have passed since Super Bowl III, and Namath has long since left center stage. Now 50, he lives in the quiet community of Tequesta, Florida, 80 miles north of the Orange Bowl, site of his epic win over the Colts. He owns a rambling, 12-room house on the Loxahatchee River, and on a warm, sunny day he likes nothing better than sitting on his private dock, fishing for snook and flounder.

He has been married to his wife, Tatiana, for eight years. They have two daughter—Jessica, 7, and Olivia, 3. He laughs about his former image as the swinging bachelor with the lavish Manhattan apartment. He reads old stories about his white llama rug and the chorus-girls-in-waiting lifestyle, and he feels as if he were reading about someone else.

"I'm a Gemini so there are a couple of me's around," Namath says, relaxing for a moment in his spacious den. "There is a mischievous side to me, and I guess being young and in New York brought that out. But my greatest pleasure now is kicking back and spending time with my family."

The knees that plagued Namath throughout his 13-year pro career have been replaced by plastic versions. He underwent the replacement surgery in April, 1992, after several incidents in which his knees, ravaged by surgery and too many games, played on painkillers and bravado, collapsed beneath him.

His greatest fear, he said, was that it would happen again one day while he was carrying his daughters, and that they might be injured in the fall.

"I feel better than I have in twenty years," Namath said. "I haven't taken any pain medication in over a year. I can walk, I can exercise on the ski machine, and I feel fine."

"Kids from the neighborhood come to the door and ask if Joe can come out and play," Tatiana says.

"I say okay," Namath says, "but on one condition: Nobody hits the quarterback."

It has been 16 years since he retired as a player, yet Joe Willie Namath remains one of football's biggest names. There were a lot of Super Bowl heroes, but there was only one brazen enough to call his shot in advance. There was only one who owned a mink coat and wore pantyhose in a TV commercial. There was only one who romanced Ann-Margaret on the silver screen. (Surely, you remember the 1969 biker movie *C.C. and Company*.)

There was only one Broadway Joe.

There still is.

"As a viewer, Joe was somebody I could relate to," says former running back O.J. Simpson, who was winning the Heisman Trophy at USC while Namath led the Jets to the AFL title in 1968. The two men were inducted into the Pro Football Hall of Fame in 1985.

"Joe came across as a real person. From his time on, fans saw football players as people. They didn't all train on milk and apple pie. I can remember Joe saying he liked his women blonde and his Johnny Walker Red. It probably made some people mad, but I liked it.

"What Joe was saying was, 'Hey, if you don't hurt anybody, it's okay to be yourself.' He wore his hair long and spoke his mind, but that's what the sixties were all about. Joe was the superstar athlete who really reflected what the younger generation was thinking."

Namath was more than just a player, he was the show that sold the American Football League. He gave the new league credibility by signing with the Jets as the top draft pick out of Alabama in 1965. The AFL had other good quarterbacks, such as Len Dawson (Kansas City), George Blanda (Houston), and Jack Kemp (Buffalo), but they all were recycled NFL backups.

What the new league needed was a star it could claim as its own. Namath was the perfect player, and New York, with its bright lights and media muscle, was the ideal setting.

David (Sonny) Werblin was the Jets' owner, and he had a background in show business. He marketed Namath the way he would a Broadway star; signing him to a $427,000 contract that made him the highest-paid player in the league.

Heads turned, jaws dropped, people took notice.

"I believe in the star system," Werblin said. "That's what sells tickets. Namath has that special stuff. Namath is DiMaggio. He's Clark Gable, Frank Sinatra, Babe Ruth."

"Namath captured the imagination of New York, and that meant the AFL captured the imagination of New York," says Art Modell, owner of the Baltimore Ravens. "It was a huge step forward. All of a sudden, here was this guy who people wanted to see, and he was in the 'other' league.

"Of course, all the publicity in the world wouldn't have mattered if Namath couldn't play. But he was the real thing—you could see that from the start."

"Namath was the best pure passer I ever saw, and he had the quickest release," says John Madden, the former Raiders head coach. "We'd put in blitzes and say, 'There is no way he can beat this.' And he would. He took some hellacious shots, but the ball was already on its way, usually for six points.

"The thing that sticks out in my mind the most about Namath is his toughness. He was one of the toughest guys who ever played the game. You read all the stories about Broadway Joe and you'd think he was a pretty boy. But he didn't play like a pretty boy. He was one tough s.o.b.

"The only time I ever went to the other team's locker room to shake a player's hand, it was Namath," Madden says. "We played the Jets in a wild game in Oakland, both teams slugging it out like a couple of heavyweights. We kept hitting Namath, he kept getting up and throwing touchdown passes.

"We won the game, and on my way out, I went to the Jets' locker room and shook Joe's hand. I'd never done that before. It was totally spontaneous. All I remember saying is, 'Hey, you're a helluva man,' and I meant it."

On the eve of Super Bowl III, Norm Van Brocklin was asked for his assessment of Joe Namath. A Hall of Fame quarterback himself, Van Brocklin was head coach at Atlanta and a firm believer in NFL superiority.

"I'll tell you what I think about Namath on Sunday night," Van Brocklin said. "After he's played his first pro game.

That was the prevailing sentiment, not only within the NFL fraternity but around the nation.

The Colts were 19-point favorites, a spread that reflected their 13-1 regular-season record and their 34-0 rout of Cleveland in the NFL Championship Game. Coached by Don Shula and boasting the game's top-ranked defense, the Colts were considered one of the great teams of all time.

The Jets were viewed as just another AFL team, which is to say one step above the sandlots. Kansas City and Oakland self-destructed in the first two Super Bowls, losing to Green Bay by scores of 35-10 and 33-14. Lombardi said the AFL representatives "didn't compare" to the top teams in the NFL.

And if Lombardi said it, it was gospel.

The Jets were a classic AFL team: freewheeling and wide open. In the 1968 AFL Championship Game, Namath and Oakland's Daryle Lamonica combined to throw 96 passes. Old-school coaches such as Lombardi and Van Brocklin called it "Mickey Mouse football."

Even the AFL's founder, Kansas City owner Lamar Hunt, had little faith in the Jets. He felt they were the weakest of the three AFL teams to appear in a Super Bowl. At 11-3, the Jets had the third best record in the league that season. Kansas City and Oakland tied with 12-2 marks in the Western Division.

"My nose was still out of joint because we [the Chiefs] weren't there," Hunt says, referring to Super Bowl III. "We lost to Oakland in a playoff, then Oakland lost to the Jets in the title game. But I thought our team and the Raiders both were better than the Jets.

"Having seen what the Colts did to Cleveland in their championship game, I really thought the Colts would beat the Jets easily."

The Jets saw the matchup differently.

Yes, the Baltimore defense was formidable, but it was aging. Namath saw the right side as vulnerable with end Ordell Braase (36 years old), linebacker Don Shinnick (33), and cornerback Lenny Lyles (32). He also knew that left end Bubba Smith took an aggressive upfield rush, which left him vulnerable to traps and draw plays.

Namath was a master at this sort of dissection. As Jets linebacker Larry Grantham said: "I don't see how any team can defense Joe. He always hits you where it hurts."

Namath made headlines even before the Jets arrived in Miami. He told reporters that, in his opinion, there were at least five AFL quarterbacks who were better than Baltimore starter Earl Morrall. Namath included himself among the five, along with his backup, 38-year-old Babe Parilli.

This caused quite a stir, inasmuch as Morrall was the top-rated passer in the NFL that season. He took over as the Colts' starter when Johnny Unitas went out with an arm injury, and he played so well that Shula stayed with him even after Unitas recovered.

Asked to respond, Morrall said: "[Namath] is getting newspaper space and that's what he's after, isn't it? Maybe he represents the kind of athlete the coming generation wants. I hope not."

During Super Bowl week, Namath exchanged words with Colts kicker and defensive end Lou Michaels at a Fort Lauderdale nightspot. What started as harmless needling heated up when Namath told the 6-2, 250-pound Michaels: "What do you know? You're just a kicker."

Michaels snarled and, as Namath recalls, "a lot of guys in tuxedos jumped in to calm things down."

Then came Thursday night, the night that forever shaped the legend of Joe Namath.

Namath went to the Miami Touchdown Club dinner to receive its Player of the Year award. As he went to the podium, a heckler—one who obviously wore NFL colors—shouted: "Hey, Namath, we're gonna kick your butt."

"I got a little hot," Namath says, looking back. "All week I read about how great the Colts were and how we didn't belong on the same field with them. I was tired of it.

"I said, 'Wait a minute, pal, I've got news for you. We're going to win this game. I guarantee it!

"I didn't plan it. I never would have said it if that loudmouth hadn't popped off. I just shot back. It was simply a gut reaction."

Jets head coach Weeb Ewbank did not hear about it until the next morning when he saw the newspaper headline: "Namath Guarantees Victory."

Ewbank was stunned. He had played along with the underdog role all week and instructed his team to do the same. The idea was to lull the Colts into thinking the game would be as easy as the oddsmakers predicted.

Deep down, Ewbank knew otherwise. He had seen the films. He knew the Colts could be beaten, but he felt making the NFL champions overconfident only improved the Jets' chances.

Everything was going fine until Namath opened his mouth Thursday night.

"I was upset with Joe," Ewbank says. "I said, 'Shula will use it against us. He'll have his players all riled up.'

"Joe said, 'Coach, if they need press clippings to get ready, they're in trouble.'"

The game took on sociological overtones. This was January, 1969. The Vietnam War had divided the country. In August, Woodstock would define a generation. The two teams were cast as metaphors for their time. The Jets, epitomized by Namath, were young and rebellious. The Colts, with their crewcut quarterbacks and NFL pedigree, were establishment.

"We took pride in being the rebels," Namath says. "A lot of our guys had long hair and moustaches. Before the game, [AFL President] Milt Woodard sent a letter ordering us to shave. He wanted to clean up our image.

"We never heard about it until after the game. Weeb never posted the letter. He knew we wouldn't go along with it."

The game played out just as Namath had expected. The Jets' underrated offensive line handled the Baltimore front four, and Namath, calling most of his plays at the line, used the power running of fullback Matt Snell (30 carries, 121 yards) to control the game.

Flanker Don Maynard had a hamstring pull, but no one outside the Jets' family knew it. Namath used Maynard as a decoy, allowing split end George Sauer to work one-on-one against cornerback Bob Boyd. Sauer caught 8 passes for 133 yards. Maynard had no receptions, yet he played an integral part in the victory.

Morrall threw 3 interceptions before Shula lifted him in the second half. Unitas came off the bench, trailing 13-0. It went to 16-0 before Unitas led the Colts to their lone touchdown with 3:19 remaining in the game.

The Jets, playing with poise and precision, made good on Namath's guarantee. They brought the AFL its first world championship. The banner headline in the *Baltimore Sun* the next day read: "Upset of the Century."

Namath's numbers were relatively unspectacular—17 completions in 28 attempts for 206 yards—but he was such a commanding figure with his play-calling and leadership that he was voted the game's most valuable player. Eleven quarterbacks have been Super Bowl MVPs, some more than once, but Namath is the only one to win the award without throwing a touchdown pass.

"I give Namath all the credit in the world," Shula says. "He backed up everything be said. We killed teams with our blitz all season, but Namath got rid of the ball so fast that even when one of our rushers came free, he still couldn't get to [Namath] in time."

"I watched the game from Carroll Rosenbloom's box," says Tex Schramm, former president of the Dallas Cowboys, referring to the late Colts owner. "It was a quiet place, let me tell you.

"We couldn't believe what was happening. We kept thinking Baltimore would turn it around. We waited and waited and then the game was over. For the [NFL] diehards—and I was certainly one of them—that game was like a punch in the stomach."

Lamar Hunt went 10 the Jets' locker room to offer his congratulations. NFL Commissioner Pete Rozelle found Hunt in the crowd and shouted in his ear: "This is the best thing that could have happened."

"Pete saw the big picture," Hunt says. "The merger was in place, the leagues were coming together, and with the Jets winning, we now had a horse race. People knew the AFL was for real."

"That game wasn't about money or individual honors, it was about respect," Namath says. "We didn't get any respect before the game. Our league didn't get any respect, period. When we won, we felt like we won for a whole lot of people, not just ourselves.

"We returned to the hotel and [Chiefs stars] Buck Buchanan and Willie Lanier were waiting for us. They wanted to say thanks. I saw [Chargers quarterback] John Hadl that night. I remember John telling me what it was like, sitting in the stands, watching us win. He had tears in his eyes.

"You ask me how much that game meant?" Namath says. "That's how much it meant."

For the Jets, the magic proved fleeting. They were beaten in the playoffs the following year by Kansas City, 13-6, starting a steep decline that lasted more than a decade.

The championship nucleus was broken up by age and injury. Ewbank stepped down following the 1973 season. Namath was sidelined with one major injury after another. He had five knee operations and was so stiff-legged under his tape and protective braces that he resembled a man playing on stilts.

"Namath was like a ghost from the waist down," says Steve Sabol, the experienced president of NFL Films. "It was as if he had no legs. If you look at film of his throwing motion, it was all upper body. He spun like a gun turret when he released the ball."

Namath was an easy target playing behind the Jets' patchwork line. Under a heavy rush each week, he took a terrible pounding. As the losses mounted, the fans began to boo. By 1976, Namath had become a forlorn figure, throwing 16 interceptions to 4 touchdown passes in a 3-11 season.

The following year, Namath was released by the Jets. The team had another young quarterback from Alabama, Richard Todd, and the plan was to build around him. Namath signed with the Los Angeles Rams, hoping he could manage one last hurrah. He struggled through four starts, then was replaced by Pat Haden.

"I knew it was time to quit when I found myself getting bored on the practice field," Namath says. "I didn't play the second half of that season. I was watching practice, and I was bored. I said, 'I don't belong out here anymore.'"

Namath retired following the 1977 season to pursue a career in TV. He did some acting and worked as a football analyst. He also performed in stage productions such as *Damn Yankees, The Caine Mutiny Court Martial*, and *Sugar*, a theatrical version of the Billy Wilder film *Some Like It Hot*.

He was inducted into the Pro Football Hall of Fame in 1985 after being passed over in his first two years of eligibility. The knock against him at the time was his statistics. His career passer rating was a mediocre 65.6. He threw 220 interceptions compared to 173 touchdown passes. He had only three winning seasons in 12 with the Jets.

To some critics, Broadway Joe was a media creation who had

one, unforgettable shining moment and little else.

Nonsense, answers John Madden.

"If there was ever a Hall of Fame quarterback, it was Namath," Madden says. "There are some guys whose numbers don't matter You don't have to count up Lawrence Taylor's tackles to know he's a Hall of Famer. He just is. Same thing with Namath.

"When you played against Namath, you knew you were playing a Hall of Famer. The whole game—everything you did, everything they did, offense, defense—it all revolved around him. He was the guy.

"I watch Dan Marino, Jim Kelly, even Joe Montana, and it is obvious they patterned themselves after Namath. The way they move, the way they throw the ball, it's like watching Namath. He influenced a whole generation of young quarterbacks, guys who have gone on to take teams to the Super Bowl.

"That's an impact player."

"Joe didn't play for stats, he played to win," Maynard says. "I see quarterbacks today throw four-yard passes on third-and-fifteen. It goes in the books as a completion, it looks good in the stats, but it doesn't accomplish a damn thing.

"I never saw Joe throw a ball short of the sticks. If he needed twelve yards for a first down, he threw it fifteen. When he got inside the twenty, he went for the end zone. He got some balls picked off, but he also made a lot of big plays that won games."

Namath's fans—and they far outnumber his detractors—sometimes wonder, "What if?"

What if Joe had played his whole career on two sound knees? What if he had played for a team that was built to last, rather than the Jets, who fell apart in the 1970s?

Namath claims he never gives it a second thought.

"Things turned out well enough for me," he says. "I'd have to be a real jerk to say, 'If only this, if only that....'

"I would've loved to win five Super Bowls, but to win one was more than most guys. Ever since Little League, my dream was to win a world championship in something. I got that chance with the Jets, and we won The Game. We touched a lot of people's lives.

"I can't tell you how many times I've had people tell me they used our win in the Super Bowl as a motivating force. A lot of times it is a high school or college coach who says he showed his team the film or told them the story. Sometimes it's a teacher who talked about it in class. The moral is the same: If the Jets did it, you can do it.

"We sent a message to all the underdogs out there—in sports, in business, in life in general—that, hey, if you want something bad enough and you aren't afraid to lay it on the line, you can come out on top. That is an important message because if people don't have hope, really, what do they have?

"People sometimes ask me, 'What would you have done if you had lost that game?'" Namath says. "Honest to God, I never even thought about that at the time. I'm sure I would have taken a lot of abuse, especially in the press, about my guarantee. But I never gave it a second thought because I was sure we would win.

"If we *had* lost, I wouldn't have run away and hid. I wouldn't have let it ruin my life. I would've come right back firing the next season. I loved the competition, that's why I played. The celebrity part was fun, I won't deny that, but the highlight of my week was game day. Strapping the gear on and playing—I lived for that."

JAY LENO

'HERE'S...JAAAY LENNNO!!'

Football insight from the host of the
Tonight Show, *or a funny thing happened*
on the way to the Super Bowl

FROM SUPER BOWL XXVII

"THIS YEAR THERE WAS a new pricing structure for the Super Bowl. The top tickets went for $1,750 each, which included a premium seat, special parking, and a celebrity brunch. Hey, for that kind of dough, I want to be able to kick off."

"What really gets me is that people will pay that much for a seat and then spend most of the time standing up and cheering—or else in line at the rest room."

"Of course, not everyone stands up during the game. Some fans are glued to their seats by all the excitement. Others are glued to their seats by the spilled soda from the guy behind him."

"Everybody who's ever played the sport has a football memory they'll never forget. Generally, it's the day they neglected to wear their cup."

"Actually, I can't understand why some fans do the things they do. For instance, they'll arrive at the game early just so they can get into the parking lot. Yet the same fans will leave the game before it's over so they can get out of the parking lot."

"Do you realize that by the end of today's game, billions of dollars will have traded hands? And that's just what the parking lot attendants will make."

"I'll never forget the first football game I went to. It was a pretty frightening experience: the brutality, the bodies colliding furiously, the sound of bones breaking. Finally, I just gave up on getting a beer and went back to watch the game."

"I wanted to have a career in sports when I was young, but I had to give it up. I'm only 6 feet tall, so I couldn't play basketball. I'm only 190 pounds, so I couldn't play football. And I have 20/20 vision, so I couldn't be a referee."

"NBC is televising this year's Super Bowl. NBC is the network that years ago brought you the famous Jets-Raiders game that was cut short for the movie *Heidi*. Remember that one? The executive who made the decision still is working at NBC. I haven't met him, but then I don't get down to the boiler room much."

"There's nothing like the thrill we Americans get at the moment of the Super Bowl kickoff. It means the pregame shows are over."

"This year, like every year, two teams will face each other in the Super Bowl. One team will win and know what it's like to be a champion. The other team will lose and know what it's like to be a Republican."

"Beer companies will spend millions just to market their products to beer drinkers during this one game. It's too bad beer drinkers are usually all in the bathroom during the commercials."

"One beer company has an interesting Super Bowl promotion. So you don't miss a minute of Super Bowl action, with every six-pack of beer you buy, you get a free box of Depends."

"As you know, the Super Bowl is very popular all over the world. This year, the game is even being televised in Russia. I bet the Russians will be oohing and aahing. Not at the game—at all those commercials for Charmin toilet paper and the Sizzler."

"Do you know why American-style football hasn't really taken off in the rest of the world? Because it's impossible to describe how big a football field is to someone who's not familiar with something 'the size of a football field.' What do you say? 'It's half the size of two football fields?'"

"Strange, but in England they think soccer is football. Of course, in England they think princes and princesses live happily ever after."

"And finally, when the Super Bowl ends, it begins a very depressing time for American men. They look around and realize that at some point during the season their wives left them."

PETE ROZELLE

TRULY THE
BIGGEST GAME

The man behind the creation of
the Super Bowl admits that not even he
thought it would get to be this big

FROM SUPER BOWL XXV

A FEW YEARS AGO, I was having dinner with Bill Granholm, a wonderful man who worked with me for decades—first with the Los Angeles Rams and then in the NFL offices. The owners had just had a rather stormy session about the future site of some Super Bowl or other. It seemed as if everything connected with the game had assumed monumental proportions.

I remember Granny picking up his cocktail, shaking his head, and saying, "Do you believe this? Do you believe this has gotten so big?"

I said "No" then and I'll say it again now. Except today it's even bigger. The stakes are even higher. For Super Bowl XXV ABC is getting $850,000 for one 30-second commercial! I don't care what kind of financial numbers you're used to, that's a staggering amount.

TRULY THE BIGGEST GAME

CBS and NBC both televised the first AFL-NFL World Championship Game (it wasn't called the Super Bowl then). CBS charged $85,000 a minute for commercials, NBC $75,000.

Assuming ABC sells out all commercial spots for XXV—which seems like a safe assumption because every game so far has—the total likely will be somewhere around $43 million.

The reason it sells out is that there is no game, no event, no show of any kind that annually reaches a larger audience than the Super Bowl. Maybe three out of four Americans, plus millions more elsewhere, are watching.

No, I never thought it would get this big. I never thought it could get this big, mostly because, well, I guess because it never occurred to us back in the 1960s.

Of course, we knew that a matchup of the champions of the National Football League and the American Football League would be a big game. We knew—or I guess we hoped—that the public would be eager to see such a square-off.

But then we got our comeuppance in the first Super Bowl when there were roughly 32,000 empty seats in the Los Angeles Coliseum. We're talking about almost 35 percent of the seats in a 94,000-seat stadium! Nine years before, in 1958, when I was general manager of the Los Angeles Rams, we averaged nearly 85,000 per game and had crowds of more than 100,000 for our games against the Baltimore Colts and Chicago Bears. (The Coliseum had a seating capacity of 102,000 in the 1950s.)

Fortunately those unsold tickets for Super Bowl I were the last empty seats we have had for a Super Bowl. It's now the most coveted ticket for any event in America.

After that first game, I remember we had a meeting to discuss the possible reasons why we hadn't sold out, A lot of people thought it was the price of the tickets. We had the tickets scaled at $12, $10, and $6. It's all relative, I know, but for the last five years, most game tickets have been priced at $100 or more. Some people resell them for 10, 20, even 30 times face value and they get it.

So we got a dose of reality in that first game. We worked hard— we had tried everything to sell seats. It was difficult to explain.

Two weeks before game I, both the AFL Championship Game in Buffalo and the NFL Championship Game in Dallas had sold out. Both the visiting teams—the Kansas City Chiefs of the AFL and the Green Bay Packers of the NFL—had won that day, setting up a game between the best teams from each league.

We couldn't have asked for a more attractive matchup, or more superstars on two teams, or two more colorful coaches—Hank Stram, the Chiefs' bantam rooster, and Vince Lombardi, the Packers' strongman.

In all my 29 years as Commissioner, except for George Halas, I was never closer to a head coach than I was to Vince Lombardi. I know it's a cliche to say that someone is a real man, but it must have been invented for Vince Lombardi. He was so strong, so powerful, so intelligent.

After the Packers outlasted the Cowboys 34-27 in the NFL Championship Game on New Year's Day two weeks before Super Bowl I, I gave Vince a call in Green Bay. He was adamant about wanting to stay in Green Bay to practice there until the Friday or Saturday before the Super Bowl, and then fly out. I told him he couldn't do that, that he had to spend the seven days or so before the game in southern California. I thought it would help sell tickets.

The Packers spent the six days before the game in Santa Barbara, and I have to say that I never saw Vince Lombardi more anxious than he was that week. The man had won four NFL championships to that point, his teams had played in five title games and countless other big games, And I know he never felt the pressure like that.

Vince knew that not only did his own ownership expect him to win, but there were 13 other NFL owners who had the same kind of emotional investment.

I was pleased that it was a close game for more than a half. I think we all feared that it might be a one-sided blowout. I was very happy with the 35-10 result.

I honestly can say that there are only three Super Bowls in which I was rooting—silently, of course—for a team. I wanted the Packers to win in both Super Bowls I and II because my NFL loyalties still were strong. And I wanted the Steelers to win in Super Bowl IX for the sake of the finest, most decent man I ever knew apart from my own father—Art Rooney.

Super Bowl II between the Packers and the Oakland Raiders was played in Miami (we played three games there in four years-II, III, and V), and Vince told me before the game that it would be his last as Packers head coach.

I guess the reality of that decision never sunk in with me because I remember being just as surprised—maybe disappointed—as everyone else when he announced his decision to step down a few weeks after the game.

The biggest stories before Super Bowl II were the rumors that he was going to quit. He never told the team directly, although he came close to breaking down in one pregame meeting, so I think they suspected it very strongly.

Like the first game, it was fairly close for a half, but the Packers came on strong in the third quarter, just as they had in January, 1967, and won 33-14.

Then came the one that I like to call the Magic Game. Game III between the Jets and the Colts not only put the Super Bowl on the map, it made it a permanent part of the American sports and entertainment consciousness.

The funny thing was that even though we had sold out game II in Miami fairly easily, we didn't sell out game III until just a few minutes before game time.

Of course, that was the game when Joe Namath went to a dinner a few days before, and, in a speech, "guaranteed" a victory over the heavily favored Baltimore team.

Even for those radical days, Joe was a pretty radical guy—one of the first players to wear his hair long, the first to wear white shoes. He was flamboyant, anti-establishment, a character.

I really did not care who won the game, but I was hoping against hope that we would have a close game. The Packers had won the first games by 25 and 19 points, and the Colts were favored by 18.

After Namath and the Jets prevailed 16-7, the NFL owners were very upset, of course. It was crushing for the old-line club people. But I was secretly pleased because I realized that this shocking turn of events was going to do nothing but help pro football.

It didn't take a brain surgeon to figure out that the Jets' victory was going to mushroom interest in our game. At that point, the merger that would be implemented after the next season was all set. By winning, the Jets proved the AFL teams belonged. Of course, as you might suspect, I never attempted to sell that logic to Carroll Rosenbloom, then the Colts' owner!

Super Bowl IV in January, 1970, at New Orleans, was the last game between the two leagues. In the 1970 season, the merger would be officially completed with realignment into two conferences.

The Vikings looked like the best team in football, but a lot of insiders said not to underestimate Hank Stram's Chiefs, who were big, fast, and talented. I thought Minnesota would win, but again, all I really wanted was a close game. Shows you what I know. It wasn't really a close game—and it was the Chiefs who won, 23-7.

For the first two years, the game officially had that unwieldy handle, the AFL-NFL World Championship Game. That was my idea. I guess coming up with catchy names wasn't something I was very good at.

Some of the press was calling it the Super Bowl from the start, but I never liked the name. To me, "super" was a corny cliche word that we used during my school days at Compton High in California in the 1940s.

The actual source of "Super" in the Super Bowl name had originated a few years before with the daughter of Lamar Hunt, the Chiefs' owner. At that time, a popular, faddish children's toy was something called a "Super Ball," which bounced dramatically higher than a regular rubber ball. Lamar's daughter had one of those balls, and he liked the name—the twist of "Super Ball" to "Super Bowl"—and he urged that we adopt it. Thankfully, we did, and game III was the first official Super Bowl.

I'm the first to admit that I was mistaken about the name of the game. "Super" takes on a different connotation when it is applied to this event. I think the name has played a big part in the game's success.

For me, there was great sadness going into Super Bowl V. In September, just before the start of the 1970 season, Vince Lombardi died after a devastating battle with cancer. Vince was 13 years older than I, but it was like losing a brother. I miss him to this day. Fittingly, the Super Bowl Trophy—that magnificent creation of Tiffany & Co.—officially was renamed the Vince Lombardi Trophy before Super Bowl VI.

Coming from a public relations background, one of my great pleasures in pro football was dealing with the media. This was especially true at the Super Bowl, particularly at the early games.

Nowadays, thousands of media people from around the world cover the game, and the closest the commissioner gets to these people is at the giant Friday noon press conference where there's a bank of TV cameras, hundreds of still photographers, and many hundreds of press, radio, and TV representatives. But in those first few years, my contacts with the media were pretty special.

I remember sitting around shooting the breeze with six, seven, eight writers at a time. It seemed to be less serious then, more fun. The game was serious, of course, but that didn't prevent us from kidding around. I have great memories of early sessions with John Steadman from Baltimore, Bob Oates from Los Angeles, Mo Siegel from Washington, Larry Felser from Buffalo, and others.

A lot of things were different in those younger days than they are today. In the early years, for example, we had no Super Bowl Site Committee the way we do now. We basically just went with our instincts, and usually that meant Los Angeles, Miami, or New Orleans. The only deviation from those cities the first 15 years was in game VII, when we played in Rice Stadium in Houston.

The only time I can recall having some reservations about the game site was when we went back to Los Angeles for game VII. Honestly, it took some courage to go back to my hometown after all the empty seats in game I, but I guess by that time we had more confidence in the game as a major event. This time we sold out the Coliseum, the major attraction being whether the Miami Dolphins could complete a perfect 17-0 season (they did).

We always have had a function of some kind for the media, and for all the people from the clubs and the league the Friday night before the game, but this didn't have the significance in the early years that it did later. In fact, before Super Bowl I, I think our "party" was nothing more than cold cuts at the Statler Hilton.

To borrow the trademark phrase of the late Ed Sullivan, I think the first really big show we had was at Super Bowl VII in January, 1973. A couple years before, the city of Long Beach had purchased the storied ocean liner, the *Queen Mary*, and had turned it into a major tourist attraction. We used the entire ship as a site for our party.

We have had some wonderful Friday night parties over the years, including some great ones in New Orleans, a party city on its own. If I had to pick a personal favorite, however, it would be the one we had before Super Bowl XXI in Los Angeles at Universal City. Being on the Universal lot in a movie studio environment was very exciting for many of the visitors.

I'm a real sucker for pageantry. I always liked balloons and balloon releases. In the early years, we also had a lot of pigeon or dove releases. I liked those, too. The fly-overs that we initiated at Super Bowl VI in New Orleans—and continued at most other outdoor Super Bowls after that—also were a big thrill.

I always was involved in our plans for pregame and halftime festivities because it seemed important to me that we make the entire *event* very special. But I usually let other people pick the person or people who would do The National Anthem. The one time I insisted on an anthem person was at game XXII when I wanted Herb Alpert to do a "pure" horn version.

Three games in New Orleans—IX, XV and XX—stand out to me for different reasons.

Game IX was the Steelers' first appearance in an NFL Championship Game of any kind after more than four decades of frustration. I am not ashamed to admit that I had tears of joy in my eyes when I presented the trophy to Art Rooney that January, 1975, day. No man ever deserved it more. Of course, I didn't realize at the time that he was going to get greedy and win three more (X, XIII, and XIV)!

On the morning of January 25, 1981, the day of game XV, I remember waking up in my room at the Hyatt Regency in New Orleans and seeing a big yellow ribbon our people had put up around the Superdome with bows above the exits. If you remember, people had been wearing yellow ribbons in support of the hostages in Iran, and those hostages were released in Tehran just a few days before Super Sunday.

Game XX between the Bears and the Patriots was memorable for a lot of reasons, most of them generated by the very colorful Bears. The sadness was that George Halas was not there to see this great victory; my good friend and an NFL founder had died two years before.

I recall my daughter Anne Marie coming back from an evening in the French Quarter wearing a "ROZELLE" headband. Late in the 1985 regular season, I had to order Bears quarterback Jim McMahon to stop wearing commercial headbands, and he reacted to this by wearing a headband with my name on it in the playoffs. Versions of that headband were big sellers in the city the week before the game.

One of the toughest trophy presentations I had to make was to Al Davis after the Raiders' 38-9 rout of Washington in Super Bowl XVIII in January, 1984. We had been enmeshed in a court battle with Al over the Raiders' move to Los Angeles in 1982. As I was leaving the room, Raiders guard Mickey Marvin tapped me on the shoulder and said, "Not everyone here hates you." That eased the pressure.

All in all, it's been a great ride—from Super Bowl I through my last game as Commissioner in XXIII to now. I wish I could literally release some balloons and doves at this point, and maybe even arrange for a fly-over for everyone reading this. You'll have to use your imagination, however. Or better, like me, keep dreaming Super Bowl dreams.

READY...OR NOT

There is nothing easy about playing
on the offensive line—especially when
the next game is the Super Bowl

FROM SUPER BOWL XXII

T HE GUARD WASN'T AWARE of waking up, but he was worrying about the reach block on the tackle in an over defense, so he knew he was awake.

He turned to find his watch on the night stand and the bed creaked. They'd moved the night before. Both Super Bowl teams had been in prominent hotels through the week, but the night before the game they both were moved into "seclusion."

"We don't know where it will be," the club guy had explained at a mid-week meeting. "But they'll move us to a small, quiet hotel the night before the game...get us closer to the stadium and away from the crowd."

The team had arrived just before 8 P.M....to find the smallish lobby of the smallish hotel full of pennant-brandishing fans.

There was another thing smallish about the secluded hotel...the beds. The guard's feet hung over the end and the elderly mattress that held his 283 pounds bowed up on each side.

It was 6 o'clock in the morning, and the California dawn was soft and golden.

"Hey, Beck...you awake?"

The guard's roommate, who played swing tackle, groaned distantly, his head half-covered by a pillow.

"No."

But the tackle stirred in his bed, pushed the pillow aside, then groaned again. "I think my back's broke. What's in these mattresses anyway, oatmeal?" The tackle was bigger than the guard.

"I don't like that reach when they go to an over," said the guard. "I don't know if I can get there quick enough."

The tackle cleared his throat loudly.

"Well, if you can't, the league's best running game and the league's best rusher are going to be embarrassed...and you'll probably get scolded."

The guard was sitting up now, toes curled against a cold tile floor.

"I ain't kidding," he said. "It's a lousy block, and I got no kind of angle."

"So it's lousy," the tackle replied, "Nothing new about that. But if you can make it, we get a chance to spring Thomas and put some serious hurt on 'em." He shrugged. "Not many people good enough to make that block, but you're one of 'em."

The Super Bowl gets media coverage of avalanche proportions, but guards usually remain relatively safe in their anonymity.

This one had until Thursday, when a TV personality did a bit with him in desperation, when the scheduled tight end wasn't available.

The TV reporter led with a question about how hard a lineman's job was.

He hadn't agreed.

The TV reporter was taken aback briefly, but pressed on.

If playing offensive line wasn't hard, what was?

He had answered by talking about his father. He'd told how his father had worked 24 years for the phone company—24 years of climbing poles to make repairs, and never mind if it was 90-degree weather or a below-zero wind chill. That, he had said, was hard...and the pay wasn't near what he made and there wasn't any crowd there, cheering, when his father did a good job.

The interview had been picked up by a network.

The guard got off the bed and limped stiffly to the bathroom. He had ripped something in his arch in week 10. There wasn't anything they could do about it until the offseason.

Offensive linemen play with injuries. You don't get beat on through preseason and regular season and playoffs without them. Playing offensive line, you get injured just as surely as you get wet when you go out in the rain.

When the guard came out of the bathroom, the tackle was snoring faintly.

This was their second trip to Super Bowl, but he still disliked the week leading up to the game. It was hard to stay normal.

It wasn't a normal game, and anybody who told you it was was crazy.

At home, the offensive line always went to dinner together on Wednesday nights. They'd done it here, too, but as soon as they'd been seated in the restaurant, people had started coming over in waves, so they ate quickly and left.

Once the game started, he told himself, they'd be fine.

And once again, he worked to ignore the niggling doubt he awakened with a short time ago.

He wondered briefly if the defensive tackle, who was in a similar hotel not far away, was awake and thinking about him.

Soon enough, though, he dismissed the defensive tackle.

"Later, baby," he said to himself.

Then he pulled on a pair of jeans and sat, barefoot, on their smallish balcony. Birds were greeting the day as he opened the black-covered folder containing their game plan and willed himself to study. He didn't hear the birds.

Discipline is the bedrock under an offensive line.

But the reach block still looked tough.

SCOTT OSTLER

CONFESSIONS OF A SUPER PIRATE

*Long ago, an inventive sportswriter
discovered that one man's coat hanger
is another man's TV antenna*

FROM SUPER BOWL XXVIII

I AM A DISTRACTION.

That is my function during Super Bowl Week. As a big-time sportswriter and member of the media, my job is to annoy the players and coaches, to distract their attention from the business of game preparation in an effort to provide reports on the mood of your favorite team.

We bring you reports like, "Today, the mood of the Buffalo Bills can be characterized as annoyed and distracted."

We are not the only distractions, of course. Among the nuisances that have been known to interfere with the players' mental focus are meals, brushing after meals, low-flying aircraft, Nintendo Game Boy, hotel maid services, and world wars.

Yet, despite the distractions, somehow the game takes place every year. Apparently, I am only a minor pain in the neck.

There was a Super Bowl, however, when I was a big pain, when I brought the pro football and TV establishment to its knees. Me and 100,000 other brave pirates.

We staged a grass-roots, rooftop insurrection that sent shock waves through the corridors of the NFL, AFL, NBC, CBS, FCC and—who knows—maybe the CIA.

We stole the Super Bowl.

It was January, 1967, and I was annoyed. Because I was a teenager then, saying that I was annoyed is redundant, but I was extra annoyed because of the Super Bowl.

Brief background: The NFL finally decided to acknowledge the existence of the upstart AFL by agreeing to a showdown championship game.

Cool! The AFL was a fun, wide-open league, exemplified by the champion Kansas City Chiefs. It would be great to see what the zany Chiefs could do against the mighty, NFL-champion Green Bay Packers. Who knows? Maybe the Super Bowl would become an annual event.

The game would be played in the Los Angeles Memorial Coliseum, and would be televised nationally by both NBC and CBS. Tickets, however, were not selling briskly. Can you imagine a problem selling Super Bowl tickets? Hello, Coliseum switchboard? What time does the Super Bowl start?

What time can you get here?

Yes, that's an old joke, but it was new in 1967.

The situation wasn't quite that bad, but the Coliseum seating capacity was 90,000-plus, and not quite 62,000 tickets would be sold. Even if a lot of the fans were overweight, the stadium would look to be a box-office bomb on TV.

To goose ticket sales, NFL Commissioner Pete Rozelle pulled the TV plug. About six weeks before the game he announced that the telecast would be blacked out in the greater Los Angeles area.

This, remember, was before satellite dishes or pay-per-view. It was buy a ticket or forget it. As a starving college student in L.A., I couldn't afford a ticket, and the nearest city that would receive the telecast was San Diego.

CONFESSIONS OF A SUPER PIRATE

A Super Bowl blackout buster!

You could get your instructions by mailing an envelope to the station. It still was two weeks before the game, but being a college student, I procrastinated for 13 days, and had to drive to the KRLA studio in Pasadena.

Years later I learned that KRLA came up with the idea six weeks before Super Sunday. "But we figured if we announced it too soon, Rozelle would black out San Diego," then-station manager John Barrett said later.

The idea was no more than a whim to the folks at KRLA, a throwaway bit of fun. They didn't understand the power of pro football. Mail poured into the station, and the phone lines were jammed with requests for antenna instructions. Everyone at the station—accountants, news directors, secretaries, janitors—was pressed into mail and phone duty for two weeks.

The demand snowballed, and the Saturday before the game KRLA deejays, including Kasey Kasem and Bob Eubanks, announced that the instruction sheet could be picked up at the station. A massive traffic jam ensued.

The station distributed about 20,000 copies of the instructions, friends passed them along to friends, and an estimated 100,000 Super Bowl antennae were lashed together and mounted on buildings across the L.A. basin.

I hurried home and set to work. The antenna consisted of five or six varied lengths of coat-hanger wire attached to a broomstick, which then was wired to your regular rooftop TV aerial.

It was so simple that a fool could put together the antenna in 20 minutes. Mine took two hours because I lacked certain tools, such as electronic aptitude. But I worked happily, humming the theme song from "Mission Impossible." The cost was about 50 cents, not counting the broom I destroyed or the $100 worth of damage to my parents' landscaping and roof suffered during installation.

I hooked it up Super Sunday morning, turned on my TV, and got pure, dazzling...snow. A quick check of the skies. No, it was not snowing over Los Angeles. The instructions said to twist and rotate the antenna until the picture came in.

Like a pilot flying through a snowstorm, desperately trying to make radar contact, I kept twisting and adjusting the antenna, while my buddy inside the house monitored the screen, until...A PICTURE! YESSS!

I felt like the villain in a James Bond movie. Try to keep me from watching your Super Bowl game NOW, Missster Rozelle. A-HA-HAHAHAHAHA!

My buddy and I kicked back with snacks and soda pop. The TV reception was not fabulous, but we definitely could tell it was a football game, even if it was hard to make out minute objects, such as the football. Had it been a color TV, we would have been able to tell which players were Chiefs and which were Packers.

No matter. What was important was that we were watching the game, and that the people of Los Angeles had delivered a message. Never again would the NFL try to black out a Super Bowl. (Of course, never again would the Super Bowl not be sold out.)

From a personal standpoint, the rest is history. Inspired by my first crude foray into electronics, I went on to invent the VCR and the microwave oven.

Just kidding. Years later I did learn to *use* a VCR and a microwave oven, though I often confuse the two. I also became a sportswriter, which means I get paid to watch Super Bowls, often from great seats, with free snacks.

Snacks? I get invited to the NFL Commissioner's Party, pal. Astronauts say that the only man-made objects visible from the moon are the Great Wall of China and the seafood buffet table at the Commissioner's Party.

But you know what? For me, the Super Bowl never will be cooler than it was in '67.

Beginning from that first fuzzy image, I became a knowledgeable, professional Super Bowl watcher. Allow me to pass along some valuable insights into viewing the game, on TV and in person.

Don't complain. Got lousy seats? They could be worse. You could be seated on one of the team benches.

It is a fascinating place from which to experience the flavor of the game—the sounds, the intensity, the Gatorade. But you have no idea what's going on. Watching a game from the sidelines is like standing way too close to a LeRoy Neiman painting.

This explains why coaches often seem confused after the game. "I was generally pleased with my team's performance, but I'll know more when I study the tapes and find out whether we won or lost."

Watch the talkers. For some reason, the players who do the most talking the week before the game almost always excel on Super Sunday. I exaggerated at the start of this piece when I said the media are a nuisance. Most players actually enjoy their daily chats with the press, and the most convivial players almost always wind up starring in the game.

Prime example: Joe Theismann in Super Bowl XVII, where he quarterbacked the Redskins to a win over Miami. That week Joe would talk your pen dry.

Focus. Don't get hung up on extraneous things. Watching one Super Bowl for example, I absentmindedly began pondering the metaphysics of the Miami Dolphins' helmets, causing me to miss five or six crucial commercials.

The Miami helmet features a dolphin wearing a tiny helmet with a 'D' on the side. Shouldn't that dolphin be wearing a Dolphins helmet, which would have a picture of a dolphin wearing a Dolphins helmet?

If the Dolphins are in the Super Bowl, make it a point not to think about this.

Update your gridspeak. Don't mark yourself as a football dinosaur by referring to passes as either "long" or "short." That confusing terminology has been greatly simplified by coaches and TV announcers. Passes now are thrown "underneath the coverage" or "up top." "Nickel package" is another handy term that can be dropped into almost any football conversation, even if you have no idea what it means.

Other useful words and phrases include: Smashmouth football, situation substitution, hang time, red zone, rotating zone, no-parking zone, speed-up offense, speed rush, foot speed, and foot fault.

Digress. If the game becomes a one-sided rout, spice up the conversation with philosophical topics. For instance, aren't you glad the NFL never has resorted to trendy singular nicknames?

The league will lose big style points in my book if it ever starts naming teams the Pittsburgh Steel, the Miami Prickly Heat (helmet: a dolphin with a rash?), the Buffalo Buffalo, or the New England Style Clam Chowder.

Ignore the QB. Novice fans focus exclusively on the quarterback and wind up missing some of the most interesting action on the field.

Try watching the guy who stands behind the head coach and keeps his headphone wire neatly coiled. This is a vital task. One slip-up and the coach could become hopelessly tangled in his own cord, unable to get out of the way of that oncoming railroad train.

Watch for a play from President Clinton. It is rumored he will resume the tradition of the U.S. President designing a play for his favorite team. Richard M. Nixon started and ended this tradition by suggesting a play to Dolphins coach Don Shula for Super Bowl VI. The play failed, and Nixon soon was demoted to private citizen.

Reminisce. People around you at the stadium—or in the bar or living room—love to hear stories about the old days.

Why, I remember when there were no end-zone nets to catch extra-point and field-goal attempts. Balls booted into the stands would touch off spirited free-for-alls.

True story: I dove into one such scrum, grabbed the ball, and tugged—only to find that I had an armlock on a bald man's head.

That couldn't happen today, of course, because of the advent of spray-on hair.

AL MARTINEZ

LET'S GET METAPHYSICAL

For a different perspective on the
Super Bowl, newspaper columnist Al Martinez
turned to the supernatural

FROM SUPER BOWL XXVII

WELCOME TO SOUTHERN CALIFORNIA.
Let me dispel any notion that you are required to be registered with an agent, a shrink or a psychic if you remain here longer than seven days. That is a rule imposed only on those associated with the entertainment industry.

An agent gets them work, a shrink keeps them working, and a psychic tells them how their dead mothers feel about it.

But agents and psychiatrists are elements of the temporal world, in contact with nothing more mystical than production companies and patients with dysfunctional libidos.

Psychics, on the other hand, open doors to, well...elevating metaphysical experiences, either through direct contact with the spirit world or by regressing us through mists of time to our past lives.

What, I hear you ask, has this got to do with football? Is there a Cosmic Bowl somewhere beyond our range of perception in which the Great Ones still go for the long bombs and where a Hail Mary takes on heavenly new significance?

On that, you'd have to check with actress Shirley MacLaine, who, as I understand it, is in constant touch with the Other Side through means not available to others. She would know about Cosmic Bowls.

All I know for sure is that the Los Angeles area abounds with people who can take you back to your past lives for an average fee of $25 a life, no checks or credit cards.

Among them is a tiny, wrinkled woman I know only as Sasha, who once took me back through a past life to where I was Yazoo, the running Indian, a champion at the game that preceded football. That is my contact with the sport and my reason, limp as it may seem, for being on this page today.

But before we get into past lives, let me explain that I always have been someone who, like Walter Mitty, was able to transport himself onto glorious planes of accomplishment through the simple medium of daydreams. I'm a mind hero. As a kid, by simply closing my eyes, I was to the old gridiron what Madonna is to showbiz, larger than life and spectacular in every respect, off field as well as on. When I scratched, thousands cheered. When I smiled, women fainted. The paparazzi trailed me everywhere.

On the field, I was beyond heroic. I was Joe Montana, Bart Starr, and Joe Namath rolled into one. I never missed. My spirals sailed through the air like angels. My handoffs were gifts from a god. In my daydreams, I was Bubba Martinez, Quarterback of the Ages.

I became so convinced that this fantasy existed that I decided to try out for high school football. It was a serious mistake. While I have since gained a few pounds (all in the wrong places) I was a skinny, jug-eared, 110-pounder in the eleventh grade at East Oakland's Castlemont High, whose football team had not lost a game in three years and whose line was heavier than that of most major universities.

Coach Roy Richert, an amiable man with a forgiving attitude, could not believe I was serious. However, he also coached track and, because of my participation the prior season in what was then the 100-yard dash, he knew I was fast—at least for the first tenth of the run. I had a terrific start that quickly faded.

"If there were a ten-yard dash in the Olympics," he said to me once, "you'd be a world champion."

At any rate, my football tryout lasted less than two minutes. He handed me a ball and said, "Run through them." *Them* was the other players, who were instructed not to tackle me but simply to stop me. I started at them with my head lowered, zigging and zagging the way Red Grange had done it. I got past a couple of players who looked at the scene as something of a big joke. But then there appeared out of nowhere a 240-pound linebacker named Barney Kaminsky with arms longer than his legs, who slapped my back with both hands in a form of, well, a killer tag. It was as if I'd been shot.

I hit the ground with a slapping sound, face down, staggered bravely to my feet, and almost instantly got sick to my stomach. It was a mess. Worse, my right arm had been underneath me when I fell, still clutching the old pigskin, and had busted just above the wrist, ending my athletic career and convincing me for all time that Bubba Martinez was safer in my head. Later, I heard my mother explain to friends that I had fragile bones and vomited easily.

But I have never given up entirely on the metaphysical, into which category daydreaming more or less falls, somewhere in the vicinity of past-life regression.

On certain lazy summer days, I still can propel myself back to the era of the Oakland Raiders and imagine I am Daryle (The Mad Bomber) Lamonica in the final 10 seconds of a game. I throw a bomb that sails 57 yards through the air while no one in the stands breathes until Fred Biletnikoff tips it into his arms with one finger and we win the game by a point.

I was raised in Oakland, you see, and began watching the Raiders in pre-Oakland Coliseum days when they still were playing on a small, makeshift field behind the Municipal Auditorium.

There was a contest to name the team when it was first created. The winner was someone who wanted to name it the Oakland Señors, but that idea crashed and burned fast, and the Raiders were born.

My heroes were Lamonica and Biletnikoff and old George Blanda and Big Ben Davidson. When I daydreamed, I could imagine myself as Lamonica and Biletnikoff and even Blanda, but Big Ben? He was 6 feet 8 inches and I am 5-9, and there are some things even I just can't dream myself up to.

I moved to Los Angeles 20 years ago and the Raiders followed 10 years later, but it was never the same. Our love affair was over at that point. They are no longer the scruffy bunch on the east side of San Francisco Bay. They are the Chardonnay Raiders, somehow daintier and more cultural in their new environment. They don't drool and growl anymore.

Back to the metaphysical, my specific interest was triggered in the 1950s when a painfully shy Colorado housewife named Ruth Simmons was hypnotized and, under hypnosis, broke into a wild Irish jig and announced she was Bridey Murphy of 19th-century Belfast.

It was the beginning of a reincarnation fad, with Bridey Murphy as the Queen of Past Lives. There was a Bridey Murphy book, Bridey Murphy cocktails, Bridey Murphy cookies, and God knows how many come-as-you-were parties.

This began a current lifelong fascination with the occult, which was the reason I began visiting past life regressionists and how I came to meet Sasha.

I had just seen the movie *Flatliners*, which was about near-death experiences and past lives, and decided to seek out someone who specialized in, as they say, the regressional arts. Sasha invited me into her dimly lit work room, ordered me into a comfortable chair, and asked if there were something personal of mine she could touch.

"Like what?" I asked suspiciously.

"Like a ring," Sasha said. She had a slight accent, which I think was contrived, and the vocal qualities of a chain saw.

She began rubbing the ring and appeared to be making some kind of psychic contact with my inner being. Later, she admitted she really didn't need the ring, it was just a prop. Skeptics required a show.

As she led me into what was supposed to be a trance-like state, her voice lost its cutting edge and dropped to the kind of soothing level that comforts babies and athletes. She bade me close my eyes and relax. She asked me to visualize a psychic tunnel and to drift through it like a leaf in an autumn breeze, backward past my birth to a former life. There were long moments of silence and then she said:

"I see an Indian. He's running. I see tents. It's a village. It is you. Your name is..." She paused several moments. "...Yazoo."

I opened my eyes. "Yazoo?"

"Close your eyes." I closed them.

"Concentrate. You are the son of a chief. I sense berries and herbs. Can you visualize anything?"

"No," I said, giving my voice the same hushed quality.

"Nothing at all?" she said irritably. Nothing.

"It doesn't matter," she said. "Your soul remembers."

Yazoo was playing a game with other Indians. Sasha wanted to know if I had ever been an athlete. I lied and said I'd played a little football in high school. I thought about Barney Kaminsky and my heart filled with hate.

"Are you angry about something?" Sasha asked.

I quickly said no and swept the image of Barney from my mind. Sasha said she saw Yazoo clearly now. He was playing a game with a ball made from the innards of an animal. An oxen, perhaps.

"My God," I whispered, "the beginning of oxenball!"

Sasha ignored my comment. She was lost in the spirit world.

"You are to carry the animal innards to a mountain top," she said. "I see bears."

"Bears?" My eyes popped open again. I closed them quickly.

"Several bears. You are to run through the bears."

"The Bears versus the Indians," I said, suddenly aware of what was going on.

"I see you running. I see a woman. You are celibate."

"It's all that damned running."

"The bears..."

She stopped.

"You can open your eyes," she said.

"What about the bears?"

"I would rather not talk about it," she said, handing me back my ring. "I'll see you some other time."

I never did find out what happened to Yazoo. I suspect the game ended Bears 1, Yazoo 0.

That was several months ago. I went looking for Sasha again for the sake of this article, but she had disappeared—no doubt in a puff of smoke—and has not been seen since.

But in the course of searching for Sasha I did find Ed Helin, a big, good-humored man in a flowered shirt who has been an astrologer for 43 years and knows something about football, having played both in high school and the Army. In fact, he lays claim to having predicted the outcome of Super Bowl XXV in front of an astrology class of 200 students several weeks prior to the game.

Astrology, which dates back about 5,000 years, even before the time of Yazoo the Indian, is the practice of interpreting the influence of planets and stars on earthly affairs in order to predict the destinies of individuals, nations, or, in this case, teams.

Ed, who has tutored celebrities as diverse as Nancy Reagan and Clint Eastwood, calls it a combination of the scientific and the artistic, with some psychic intuition thrown in for good measure.

The practice has many doubters, including those who dismiss it as so much Taurus do-do—Taurus being, of course, the Zodiac bull. When journalist H.L. Mencken, a noted skeptic, once was asked how he felt about moon and sun signs, he replied, with characteristic wit, "The other day a dog peed on me. A bad sign."

Ed shrugs off the skepticism by saying to those who regard astrology as an impossible pastime that, scientifically and aeronautically, it is also impossible for bumble bees to fly. But they do it just the same. While the parallel may lack Mencken's sting, you get the point. Big Ed believes in the stars.

He takes credit for having predicted not only the outcome of Super Bowl XXV but also the tightness of the game and the failure of a last-minute field-goal attempt by the Buffalo Bills, which gave the contest to the New York Giants by a score of 20-19.

When I asked him to figure the fortunes of Super Bowl XXVII, he turned to his Digicomp DR-70. The Digicomp is a miniature computer. I realize it's a disappointment, but they don't use quills and scrolls anymore. The DR-70 churns out a hard copy of numbers and astrological symbols in seconds.

Ed punched in the date and approximate starting time of Super Bowl XXVII and, using computations he had already assembled, said it looks good for the American Football Conference. "Looks good" and "seems like" are phrases astrologers employ to leave an escape valve for predictions that go awry.

But Ed was nonetheless forthright when it came to calling today's winner. Bear in mind first that I'm writing this in mid-November, so his predictions are done from something of a distance. But that didn't bother Nostradamus, an astrologer who lived almost 500 years ago and whose prophecies are still being honored by students of the occult. Nostradamus, alas, didn't predict the outcome of Super Bowl XXVII, so we are left to rely on Big Ed.

Ed believes that today's game is being played between the Houston Oilers and the San Francisco 49ers and that Houston will win it 24-10. The reason for that is the AFC is ruled by Capricorn and the NFC by Cancer and there are more power planets on the Oilers' side than on the side of the 49ers.

The stars further reveal to Ed that the Oilers' game plan will be unorthodox and full of surprises and, because of the presence of Neptune, is not above including what he calls "sneaky plays."

However Ed's predictions turn out, this much you can count on. I'll be there today, down on the field. I will be the wide receiver, 6-foot-5, a thing of grace and beauty who will leap toward the blue sky and pull a pass from the heavens with fingertips of gold to win the game in the last 10 seconds and imprint my name in the record books for all time to come.

Eat your heart out, Kaminsky. Look at the old guy now.

EUGENE McCARTHY

HE WAS OF A DIFFERENT KIND

When the great Johnny Blood
(McNally) entered a room, everyone
knew someone special was present

FROM SUPER BOWL XXVI

TWO DECADES AGO a sportswriter asked nine leading American historians and social and cultural commentators, "What is the role of the National Football League in American history?" Of the nine experts who responded to the sportswriter's inquiry, only one found any positive social or cultural good coming out of the NFL, in or after its first 50 years of existence. The views of the other eight ranged from those who said they had no ideas about the league's influence on history and no interest in trying to find out, to the absolute and final judgment of historian Henry Steele Commager, who said that the NFL had "no importance whatsoever."

One gets the impression these same experts might very well have given the same answers had they been asked to evaluate the effect of poetry on American history in the same 50 years. One might say of football, as W. H. Auden said of poetry, that "it makes nothing happen," but it survives in its own way, a "happening." The judgment of the immediate experts obviously was different from Auden's judgment of poetry. Perhaps they were too farsighted to see football's effects on contemporary historical and cultural realities, or their insights too penetrating to note the obvious. The influence of football, like that of poetry, is not obvious or superficial or broadly social, but subtle and personal.

It provides lasting memories of personal triumphs and failures, and also of team victories and losses, whether the experience is in sand-lot, high school, college, or professional games.

When a football player rises to thank his coach and his teammates at a victory or an award banquet, he gives proper credit. When a player does the same at a baseball or basketball function, such thanks often must be taken as partly ritualistic.

The experience of football, either by players or spectators, always must be weighed upon the scales of individual experience and team experience. Vicarious satisfaction of the spectator is more complete than that attained from watching most other sports. It can be measured and observed in a fixed frame of time and space. The field is measured, length and width, not projected within the extended lines of right triangle, as is the case with a baseball diamond, nor is the size of the field variable among different levels of competition, as is a basketball court or a hockey rink. A baseball game theoretically may last forever. Time is not "taken out" in baseball but "called." It might never come back. In football, quarters are measured. Time outs are taken, for minutes or seconds. Plays must be started within fixed time limits.

Football players and their fans clearly remember great plays, great games, and players who were great, if only for a day, or less. Several years ago I visited a friend who had been in college with me 50 years earlier. He was dying of cancer. I remembered him as a freshman in his first intrasquad practice game. He ran the opening kickoff through the varsity—a championship team of the previous season—for a touchdown. In the end, however, he never made the team. On that day I saw him in the hospital, he said,

"That was a high moment of my life. I didn't know that anyone had seen that run or remembered it." He died soon after.

After all the heroes of the past and present have been talked about, all the great games and plays recalled and retold, the name of Johnny Blood (McNally) is spoken. It is like the names of the Irish patriots of whom the poet Yeats wrote:

They were of a different kind
The names that stilled your childish play
They went 'round the world like wind.

The power of his name was strong and very much alive when I went to St. John's University in Minnesota in the 1930s. John McNally played his college football at St. John's in the 1920s. He enrolled in 1920. In his three years at St. John's, he won three letters each in football and basketball, two in track, and two in baseball. It was while playing college sports at St. John's that he began his professional football career, and took on his professional name of Johnny Blood. The often-told story of the change of name is that he took it from the title of the movie *Blood and Sand* as a cover while he was playing semipro football in Minneapolis—at the same time he was playing collegiate football at St. John's.

Limited athletic achievement can take on significant proportions for public figures. After I got to the Senate, it was reported that I had been scouted as a first baseman by the Chicago White Sox, or reported accurately that I had been the high scorer on the St. John's hockey team in a championship year, and that I had played against the great goalie Frankie Brimsech, of later fame as "Mr. Zero" with the Boston Bruins. The response to these statements, claims, or admissions was nothing compared to the reaction, when, with modesty and truth, I reported that I had played end on a team that included John McNally's brother Jim at the opposite end. The team was the college sophomore intramural team. The McNally connection was magic.

Johnny Blood played 21 years of professional football, 14 of them in the National Football League. He was one of the original 17 players inducted into the Pro Football Hall of Fame in 1963.

People who knew Johnny Blood thought about him, tried to understand him, and then attempted to speak or write about him both before and after his death.

In 1955, Ernie Nevers, a former teammate, said, "When I think of Green Bay, I think of Johnny Blood. Offhand, I'd say he was the most unbelievable character in pro ball."

When John Kennedy met McNally for the first time, during the Wisconsin Presidential campaign of 1960, he said, "Your name was a household word in our home."

In a 1963 tribute to McNally, U.S. Supreme Court Justice Byron White wrote, "Not only was John a magnificent player and a brilliant entertainer, but he had the rarest of all qualities, namely, giving his greatest performances when the greatest was required. This, of course, is the hallmark of the great athlete, and it is also one of the major tests which time applies to the deeds of men."

"There never was a guy in football like Blood—never," wrote Oliver Kuechle of the *Milwaukee Journal*, following Blood's death in 1985. "All who ever played with him agree—the Cal Hubbards, the Lavvie Dilwegs, the Bo Molendas, the Cecil Isbells, the Don Hutsons, an impossible lot of contemporaries at first glance, perhaps, but really not impossible at all, for Johnny Blood's course ran through the National Football League for fourteen years."

As a special tribute to Johnny, the NFL, which prohibits the use of false names in its records, made an exception. He is remembered forever as "Blood," with parentheses for the unknowing so that there may be no confusion, and that all who read shall know that the "two in one" is Johnny Blood (McNally).

Johnny returned to St. John's in 1950 as a student, 30 years after he had rejected Notre Dame and Dartmouth and gone to St. John's the first time. He became a professor and coach. His problem as coach, it was said, was that he designed his offense and defense as though he were playing every position.

As a professor, his interests ranged from football to philosophy and literature. Captain Ahab in his contest with Moby Dick, Johnny observed, "had the courage of ignorance, comparable to the courage of a fullback playing his first season of professional football."

EUGENE McCARTHY

When I took a run at the Democratic nomination for President as a Senator from Minnesota in 1968, Johnny Blood helped lead the interference for me. For years after that—and especially in 1972—he traveled around the nation telling people they should vote for me. Some of his travels I heard about years later.

Johnny summed up his philosophy of life, and the role of football in his life, in these words: "There are literally thousands of different ways that people can express themselves. It's dazzling how many different gifts are locked up in the genes of the human race. And some people have the gift of football. That is what they can do. And they will do it whether you pay them or not."

Football was Johnny Blood's gift.

I last saw him at the Touchdown Club awards dinner in Washington, D.C., in January, 1977. The St. John's University team had won the national small college championship and its coach was John Gagliardi, who had succeeded McNally as coach 24 years earlier. In the midst of giving out awards, introducing stars, owners, and other notables, someone at the head table noticed John, at the rear of the room. He had come uninvited and unannounced to be there while his school was honored.

When his name was called, he reluctantly stepped out into the spotlight, tall, ascetic looking, white haired, in a black rain coat. A strange silence fell upon the crowd. It was as though both those who knew who Johnny Blood was, and those who did not, sensed that someone different and special was present. The applause was restrained, reverent, prolonged.

Someone had come back from another time—a knight errant of medieval times, or one of the heroes of Irish mythology, Finn, perhaps, or better Cuchulain, of whom an Irish bard wrote:

They gazed with mournful wonder on his eyes
As Spring upon more ancient skies
While all about the harpstrings sang his praise
And Conchubar, the King, with his own fingers
touched the brazen strings.

AUGUST WILSON

HERO WORSHIP ON SUNDAYS

When even the great Jim Brown turned
out to be human, novelist August Wilson
learned that all things are possible

FROM SUPER BOWL XXVI

THE SUPER BOWL has become so much a part of American popular culture that it is difficult to imagine or remember a time before there was a Super Bowl, when the price of a Broadway theater ticket was anywhere from $2 to $10 and you could see your local professional football team for $3.90. A time before cable TV and VCRs and microwave ovens. A time before *Monday Night Football*, when all the games were played on Sunday afternoons, and Sunday evenings were dedicated to Ed Sullivan, watched on 19-inch black-and-white televisions. This was before the Beatles, Bob Dylan, or the Supremes. This was years before you could transport an entire football team, its staff, and 200 fans on the same airplane, and long before anyone ever had heard of Bill Gates or Microsoft, back when the letters DOS might have stood for Defensive and Offensive Strategy. It was a time when

86

professional football was played on grassy fields, though with the same skill and intensity with which it is played today.

In 1959, I was 14 years old and lived in Hazelwood, a working-class area of Pittsburgh made up mostly of steel workers who worked at the Jones and Laughlin Steel mill. On Saturdays, they drank beer and cut their lawns, and on Sundays, they took their wives and daughters to church. Their sons, it seemed for the most, were left to their own devices.

Sports in Hazelwood was a pretty serious proposition, and almost every kid had the opportunity to play for one team or another. These teams were started and sponsored and supported by stout men with large hands and broad backs who sought ways to teach their sons rules of conduct and ideas of fair play, and to instill in them a competitive spirit that would serve them well when they grew up and became lawyers or shoe salesmen or advertising executives. Sports might even lead to college and a job other than the arduous and all-consuming work of making steel.

To a 14-year-old in a world of rapidly shifting values and expectations, sports is more a way of discovering than defining yourself, of testing and exploring the limits of potential. A way of being and becoming. It is a world unto itself, and nothing is as important within that world as its heroes. Every home run by Hank Aaron and every knockout by Sonny Liston became a victory for you, an announcement of your presence in the world, flush with an exciting armada of possibilities. You lived through your heroes.

In the minds of the boys I grew up with, no one loomed larger as a hero than Jim Brown, who had blazed his way into our consciousness in 1957. Jim Brown, was everything we wanted to be. Big, quick, and powerful, he ran right over the linebackers, leaving would-be tacklers scattered like bowling pins. He stood head and shoulders above any other running back playing the game. He was, in a word, magnificent. As we were. Or wanted to be. And could be through him. Every 100-yard game, every touchdown was a salute to our possibilities. We named ourselves after him and argued our right to do so.

This year, 1959, also was the year when we, as incoming freshmen, began our sports careers at Gladstone High School. The baton was passed to us to avenge the litany of crushing defeats suffered at the hands of Westinghouse High School, the powerhouse perennial city football champions. We doubted we could beat them, but we took a solemn vow that we would not be beaten 66-0, we being Earl, Jesse, myself, and Ba Bra (pronounced Bay Bra, short for Baby Brother), whose real name was Arthur.

On a crisp autumn morning (what other kinds of autumn mornings are there?), the four of us rendezvoused at Earl's house to begin an adventure that has stayed with me for 32 years. We were determined to see Jim Brown and the Cleveland Browns play the Pittsburgh Steelers, despite the fact we had all of $2 among the four of us. Familiar with the security at Forbes Field, which we tested (sometimes successfully) during innumerable Pittsburgh Pirates baseball games, our plan called for an early arrival, long before the ticket-takers and the small army of security, vendors, ushers, and other official personnel took their places. A short walk from Hazelwood, along Second Avenue up the winding road into Oakland, would put us at the foot of the 15-foot wall that surrounded the stadium. Though we never had done it before, we did not for a moment doubt our ability to scale even a 30-foot wall to see the great Jim Brown.

The four of us were friends, comrades, neighbors who lived on the same street, fell in love with the same girls, and learned, each in his own way, the same things. We also were each others' nemeses and delighted in our small victories. Earl was the tallest, Jesse the strongest, Ba Bra the fastest, and I was the best all-around athlete. Nobody could hit a baseball farther than me, nobody could throw a football like Ba Bra (a beautiful spiral that was deadly accurate; he was the presage, both in size and temperament, to the gifted Joe Gilliam), nobody could block shots or hook a basketball better than Earl, and nobody could catch a baseball or a football more skillfully than Jesse. We were good kids with a strong sense of community. We cut lawns, washed the neighbors' cars, and made yearly expeditions to a hidden and abandoned apple orchard, learning the location of which was in itself a rite of passage.

There we picked bushels of apples that we sold for $3 to get enough money to buy a pair of $7.98 Converse tennis shoes.

Our conversation up the winding road probably was about football, Jim Brown, and the dreaded confrontation with Westinghouse High School, which followed us everywhere like a gathering storm.

At 10 a.m. the security guards were nowhere to be found, and the wall proved difficult, but somehow surmountable. Finding ourselves alone among 35,000 empty seats, we took the best seats in the house and waited for the game to begin. The best seats in the house proved to be too visible and when the security guards went on duty, we eventually were spotted. But Forbes Field was a large place, and we ran and took seats in the third deck until the gates opened and the crowd began to arrive.

It never occurred to us that the game would be sold out, and every time we settled into a seat someone would come to claim it, until ultimately we were forced to watch the game standing up in the aisles, ducking ushers. And watch it we did.

What a magnificent spectacle! It was big and it was beautiful and it was alive. It was number 32, the Great One himself, now carrying for a 6-yard gain, a 12-yard gain, a 3-yard gain, an 8-yard gain. And then, somewhere in the middle of the game, it happened. To the best of my recollection, what happened was this: Jim Brown broke a 73-yard run. On a quick burst up the middle, he ran over a linebacker and shook off two or three would-be tacklers on his way down the sideline, where some brave defensive back risked life and limb to save the touchdown by lunging and grabbing him by his ankles 2 yards short of the goal line. Now maybe I have embellished this over the years. Often in the retelling of an event, we exaggerate it until we ourselves come to believe it, to the point where we no longer can separate fact from fiction. So I concede beforehand that some football historian, some NFL statistician, some discriminating fan or sportswriter may prove that it was a 43-yard run, or maybe a 37-yard run, but what happened next is indisputable and irrefutable.

We held our breath and secretly prayed in the name of poetic justice that Jim Brown be given the ball so he could score the touch-down he had so narrowly missed. The dictates of poetic justice pre-vailed and the handoff went to Brown who, while negotiating the 2 yards into the end zone, did the unspeakable. He fumbled.

We were, to a man, crushed. It is not an easy thing at 14 years old to see your hero falter. Not that we were unaware that fumbles and missteps were part of the game. We had seen Roberto Clemente drop a fly ball, and we had seen Hank Aaron strike out. But somehow this was different. This was bigger. Maybe because no matter how brilliant the run, it was incomplete and needed the 2 yards to legitimize it. Maybe, and I think this is more accurate, we simply had invested too much of ourselves in Jim Brown's heroics. Whatever it was, our spirits were bruised, and as we be-gan the walk back down the winding road, the fumble stayed with us. It hung in the air, unspoken. We walked in silence and gradu-ally it came to us: The possibility of failure carried with it the pos-sibility of success. If the great Jim Brown could fumble the ball, then maybe just maybe, the great Westinghouse High School football team could stumble on its way to the championship. It was a thought where there had been none before.

"Hey, man, you think Westinghouse take City again this year?"

"I don't know. They ain't so tough. They only beat Carrick by twenty-six points."

"If you don't be scared...Half the time that's how they win, 'cause the other team be scared."

"We got a good defense. All you got to do is stop Henderson. He the one be scoring all their points."

"Hey, Earl."

"What?"

"Why you got such a big head, man?"

"Yeah. And look at them feet."

"I don't know how you walk with them size twelves."

We turned onto Second Avenue, the wind at our backs and the road home welcoming us as heaven welcoming a saint.

PHIL BARBER

LXII: FOOTBALL IN FUSION AGE

If you think the current-day Super Bowl
is an extravaganza, wait until
you read about what lies ahead

FROM SUPER BOWL XXVI

R IO DE JANEIRO, February 21, 2028—Could any conclusion to any event have fit better? After two wacky, tumultuous weeks in a city that had gone certifiably *louco* over a football game, could any concluding image have been more appropriate than a loose ball bouncing freely, if erratically, toward an un-manned end zone? For evidence of the game's dramatic nature, take a look at the Super Bowl LXII highlight compilation, which NFL Films had put onto magnetic reso-disc and packaged before most of the fans had boarded the monorail.

From the moment one stepped into the Rio heat and realized that, yes, February is a summer month in South America, it was obvious this would be a Super Bowl like no other. From the tiny NFL shields that Brazil had sewn onto all national flags to pro-mote the game to the giant football scenes projected onto the surrounding mountains at night, the developing giant spared few flourishes.

Perhaps the most amazing sideshow at Super Bowl LXII was the "NFL in Yo' Face" attraction at Disney World Rio, where the league held its gigantic party Friday night. Of course, everyone had seen the advertisements for this billion-dollar creation, but few could have been prepared for it. Just to suit up in the authentic NFL uniform of one's choice satisfied a nearly universal deep-seated desire, but the full production was unreal. A mixture of film images, real-life game sounds (and smells), and actors portraying savage defensive linemen, it was the closest most of us ever will get to taking a snap against an NFL defense. It was so realistic, in fact, that I was charged with intentional grounding on a crucial third-down play.

But it wasn't the fanfare, diverting as it may have been, that made this particular Super Bowl week so memorable; it was the two teams involved, the conference champions. This was the ultimate clash of worlds: the high-tech Hong Kong Dragons, the first team to train completely underwater, versus the blood-and-guts Los Angeles Raiders, who still wear silver and black as other teams move to fuchsia and mauve. The far-flung Eastern (Hemisphere) Conference against the Western Conference, made up primarily of long-time NFL teams. New versus Old. The Offense of the '30s vs. the Defense of the '20s.

The week-long interview process, conducted wholly through two-way closed-circuit television, was almost as colorful as the face-to-face press conferences of old. In only a limited number of cases was the plug pulled because of a displeasing query.

The star of Super Bowl week was Hong Kong's Takehiko Tsuchiya, the latest NFL head coach to be described as a "genius." Admittedly, the label isn't far from the mark this time. Born in Japan, educated at Tokyo University, Oxford, and MIT, Tsuchiya claims he "never watched a complete football game" until he worked on a certain doctoral thesis, an analysis of motion and force that concentrated on wide receivers being pummeled while running crossing patterns.

Since the completion of that project, Tsuchiya has thought about little other than football. Using his own copyrighted software programs to break down every NFL game of the last 25 years play by play, Coach T. claims to have determined the ideal formation and play for every conceivable situation, against any opponent.

"After running through 500,000 simulations of the game," he declared to an astonished press corps on Tuesday, "I have concluded that we will win 27-21...or possibly 30-21, depending on whether my kicker converts a third-quarter field-goal attempt. In addition, we will outrush the Raiders by 120-130 yards, and will hold an approximate two-to-one lead in time of possession."

"Why even play the game?" one reporter teased.

"The international television and sponsorship rights were negotiated long ago," Tsuchiya replied without smiling.

The coach's conclusions would have sounded like wild rantings, of course, had his team not soundly thrashed the NFL competition throughout the 2027 season. The Dragons, after finishing the regular season 18-2 and setting a league record with 249 rushing yards per game, were being compared to the greatest teams in NFL history, storied casts such as the '78 Steelers, the '89 49ers, the '03 Patriots, and, yes, even the '17 Conquistadores.

The Raiders, in contrast, stumbled and staggered a few times along the way to a 14-6 regular-season record. But after their 24-14 victory over "North America's Team," the rejuvenated Dallas Cowboys and their Doomsday V Defense, it was clear Los Angeles was a team to fear. The Raiders' catalyst, of course, is young Wingin' Willie Wadholm-Jermain, who became the first NFL quarterback ever to surpass 7,500 passing yards (7,584) in a single season in 2027. It was only four years ago that Wadholm-Jermain led the Canadian football team to a gold medal in the 2024 Winter Olympics, and his legend has mushroomed ever since.

Though most of Wadholm-Jermain's teammates are too young to remember Al Davis, Ken Stabler, Howie Long, and the other Raiders of bygone eras, they seem to be cut from the same idiosyncratic mold. They curse, spit, and laugh just like Raiders always have, and apparently always will.

LXII: FOOTBALL IN FUSION AGE

Another indication of how much things stay the same: Who but the Raiders would appoint the NFL's first female head coach? The decision to promote Dawn Shula-Rodriguez from offensive coordinator two years ago was met with reaction ranging from hearty applause to snickering. Men's rights groups even protested. But there can be little debate now as to whether Ms. Shula-Rodriguez inherited any of her grandfather's coaching genes. (Don Shula retired in 1999 as the winningest coach in NFL history.)

Shula-Rodriguez also has managed to retain her sense of humor under tremendous pressure. When asked Thursday if she had devised a new game plan to combat Tsuchiya's Fusion Age attack, she replied, "Yeah, we've installed the Run-and-Shoot," a tongue-in-cheek reference to the long-outmoded offense popularized in the 1990s.

The venue itself was a topic of much conversation as the game approached. The Brazil Dome—*O Domo Brasileiro*—is a model for all future super-stadiums. To put 118,000 spectators in comfortable pivoting seats, all of which provide good views of the on-field action, is impressive enough. But to think that the electricity for the arena—from the lighting to the heightened-resolution scoreboards to the card scanners at the merchandise stands—is completely solar-generated is to try the imagination.

The outside world first was treated to a glimpse of *O Domo* during the 2026 World Cup soccer finals (won by the upstart U.S. team, as if you needed a reminder), but the accommodations have gotten even better in the short time since. Each seat now is equipped with a personal video monitor that allows the fan to view the game action from his or her choice of camera angles, along with slow-motion replays of every down. Finally, the comforts of the living room, minus a robotic foodserver, in the midst of a cheering throng.

Of course, the Brazil Dome wasn't the only stadium filled to capacity on Super Sunday. As were the last few Super Bowls, this year's game was played "live" in the home arenas of the two participating teams. Well, almost live—as the real Super Bowl LXII battle was waged here, holographic images of the game action simultaneously were beamed onto the fields of the Los Angeles Coliseum and Hong Kong's Giant Olive.

Kickoff, if you remember, originally had been scheduled for 4 P.M., Rio de Janeiro time, but was moved to 5:30 when a long-range forecast indicated ultraviolet radiation would be "heavy to unhealthful" about noon, when many fans would have been enjoying the exhibits outside the stadium.

The schedule change made it easy for all fans to be in their seats for the pregame festivities, which were highlighted by a musical extravaganza called, "Jump Back! The Godfather Turns 100." It was a rollicking tribute to James Brown, born in 1928. An address by NFL Commissioner Tony Gonzalez—who joked about his former team, the Kansas City Chiefs, failing to repeat as Western Hemisphere champion in 2027—was followed by the National Anthems of the United States and Brazil, both performed by Old Kids on the Block. Many an eye misted as 55-year-old Donny thanked the audience for being a part of the Old Kids' worldwide reunion tour.

Then came the coin toss. When Roger Staubach, 86 years old and still looking fit as a midshipman, strode across the field to greet the 10 or 12 team captains and decide possession of the opening kickoff, the whole event took on a different perspective, at least for me.

Could it really have been 50 years ago that Staubach led the Cowboys to a 27-10 victory over the Denver Broncos in Super Bowl XII? I was only 13 years old at the time, but I remember the game well. Thinking about it set my mind wandering through the many changes the game of football has experienced over the last five decades.

For instance, Super Bowl XII was the first one played indoors, at the original Louisiana Superdome. Yesterday's game also took place under a roof, but back in January of 1978 that meant an artificial surface. It was long before we learned how to grow natural grass indoors, before AstroTurf was outlawed. I remember joining those voices that harped about artificial turf, now I almost would say that I miss it, if only for the sake of nostalgia.

LXII: FOOTBALL IN FUSION AGE

Of course, the equipment has changed dramatically. Gone are the hard-plastic helmets, bulky pads, cage facemasks, and relatively loose-fitting uniforms of the seventies. The NFL player of 2028 would sooner play with radioactive waste than take the field without his lightweight titanium helmet, skin-tight latex uniform equipped with durable airbags, and form-fitting cleats with built-in ankle wraps. And in-helmet radios for sideline-to-field communication? They would have seemed like science fiction back in '78.

The players have changed, too. Despite what most old fogies such as myself will tell you, today's players are bigger, stronger, and faster than those of my childhood. Sure, with 55 players on each active roster, they can afford to be more specialized as well (Dragons linebacker Tex Hager enters the lineup only on third-down plays with between 8 and 12 yards to go for a first down), but consider this comparison: The Cowboys' heaviest offensive lineman in Super Bowl XII was center John Fitzgerald, who weighed 260 pounds; the Raiders' starting offensive line for Super Bowl LXII *averaged* 335 pounds.

In 1977, footballs still were made of leather; assistant coaches numbered eight or nine per team, as opposed to the 21 on the Dragons' sideline yesterday; the goal posts were much wider (they were narrowed from 18 feet 6 inches to 12 feet 6 inches in 2018, when field-goal percentages routinely creeped above 90); and, gasp!, there was *no such thing* as instant replay in officiating. Who among us NFL fans would be brave enough to live without subjection to review now?—although, with sensors on the ball and laser beams across each sideline, goal line, and end line, plus another at the first down marker, the replay official doesn't get involved as much as he once did.

We interrupt this sentimental flashback to bring you...halftime! A lot of people thought last year's production at Wembley Stadium—a lifelike re-creation of the bombing of London during World War II—was the ultimate halftime show, but LXII's might have been its equal. This year's included a salute to the joint U.S.-Japanese space program, complete with 200 antigravity gymnasts and a working model of the manned capsule scheduled to blast off for Mars in 2030. More appropriate to the South American setting was a traditional ceremony by native Guarani dancers.

For highlights of the game itself, please turn to one of the 40 or so other Super Bowl stories in this NewsMail. Anyway, you probably were watching as closely as I was at the end of the fourth quarter when, despite a large advantage to the Dragons in yardage, first downs, and time of possession, the score was tied at 17-17. You probably witnessed the scene as Dragons quarterback James Kaplan-Lopes-Baban dropped back to pass with the clock winding down and was hit by two Raiders defensive ends at once, the ball squirting free and bouncing into the Hong Kong end zone, where Los Angeles linebacker Nik Pontino fell on it for the winning score.

Moments later, the game was over, and the ecstatic Raiders dumped a tub of kelp-and-pollen liquid protein supplement over the head of Shula-Rodriguez. Still damp in the locker room afterward, she said, "The only hard drives that win football games are in the heart, not in a computer."

What a coach! What a woman! Maybe we'll see her at Carnival next weekend.

Notes: The ratings for the Global Broadcasting Company's telecast were tabulated immediately after the game, and the worldwide audience was estimated at 1.45 billion. The American television audience was placed at 204,312,000, making Super Bowl LXII the third-most-watched program in United States history, behind games L and LVII. Nine of the all-time top 10 broadcasts have been Super Bowls, the sole exception being the farewell episode of *The Simpsons* in 2011...The capacity in-stadium crowd consumed approximately 33,000 soy dogs, 40,000 bags of peanuts, 24,000 *churraquinhos*, 7,500 iguana burgers, 13,000 gallons of water, 8,000 gallons of soft drinks, and 13,000 gallons of Chug beer substitute.

PETE HAMILL

FROM BROOKLYN TO MONTANA

It never is too late to learn about
football, author Pete Hamill says, or
about the lessons the game teaches us

FROM SUPER BOWL XXIX

I NEVER WAS MUCH of a football fan when I was a kid, for a very simple reason: I never played the game. The reasons for this were not so simple. One was economic. I grew up in a Brooklyn slum, where the Great Depression lingered for years. We played stickball, using bats made from broom handles and a pink tennis ball called a Spaldeen. We boxed in the local Police Athletic League gym. We played softball without gloves or spikes. There were school yards for handball and basketball.

Football was an expensive game to play. Helmets, shoulder pads, jerseys, and cleats all cost money. There was no football team at my grammar school, where equipment might have been supplied. Neither was there at my high school. In the streets, we played occasional games of touch football with a "ball" made of wadded newspapers lashed together with tape. But football—real football with real equipment—wasn't part of our lives.

In addition to cost, there were more subtle reasons. In the years after the war, football was still a college game. We knew that Army played Navy each winter, and of course, every good Irish-American boy was urged to cheer, cheer for ol' Notre Dame. But in that blue-collar America, few of us went on to college; it took the GI Bill to break down down those barriers of class and tradition. For us, football was part of some distant boola-boola country of raccoon coats and hip flasks and fraternities. It was as distantly removed from our lives and our passions as tennis and golf.

Some high schools did play football, of course, and there were sandlot teams. But as a boy, I was discouraged from even thinking about playing football. My father, an Irish immigrant, played soccer in the New York immigrant leagues in the mid-1920s. One afternoon in 1927, he was kicked hard in the leg, suffering a double compound fracture. By the time the surgeons got around to him— this was the era before penicillin—gangrene had set in. His left leg was amputated, and his life was permanently changed.

American football and soccer weren't the same, of course, but the American game was just as dangerous. There was no hard family prohibition against playing the American game. But it was clear from my father's passions that it was better to dream about being Jackie Robinson or Willie Pep.

And there was another reason: I grew up before television. Baseball came to us through radio. Red Barber and Connie Desmond (and, later, Vin Scully) made the Dodgers live in our imaginations before we ever saw them in the lost green pastures of Ebbets Field. Nobody performed that task for football. There were football games on radio, but the game was somehow too technical, too fragmented, to blossom in a kid's imagination. Besides, it was a winter game. In the fierce winters of the years after World War II, we always dreamed of summer.

So I came late to football, and it took television to open the door. Even in the primitive black-and-white images of the late 1950s, I could appreciate the craft of a man such as Y.A. Tittle. As the quarterback for the New York Giants, Tittle became a distinct personality: balding, battered, tough in the quiet style of the era. If he was hurt, he didn't whine; pain was part of the game. If he was losing, his face said that he still thought he could win. In memory, he's always backing up in a snowstorm, and the Packers are charging. Tittle didn't make me a fan, but he gave football a face.

After that, the faces became more familiar: Charlie Conerly and Sam Huff, Andy Robustelli and Kyle Rote, Frank Gifford and Johnny Unitas. They weren't famous because they were photographed; they were famous for what they did. When I first saw Jim Brown, the Cleveland Browns' incomparable running back, I knew I was watching one of the greatest athletes who ever lived. And then there was Joe Namath.

Broadway Joe, laughing through the pain, brilliant on the playing field, moved through the night side as if he would be young forever. There he was on the hard Sunday fields, his legs as stiff as my father's, with every play representing a new risk to his career. And there he was coming in the door of the saloons, snow melting on his mink coat, laughing and nodding, a girl on his arm and another one at the table.

Namath was as important to his time as Muhammad Ali, at once elegant and brash, saying what he was going to do and then doing it. Namath showed again that, in sports as in life, will is infinitely more important than talent. He legitimized his team and his league, the old AFL, and more than any other player, he transformed the Super Bowl into a national event instead of a postseason payday.

Watching these athletes, I began to understand the game. And the roles of the players. Not just the backs. But the men on the line. Coaches were important, but in a game that mirrored war, it was clear that nobody could win without the infantry.

Television let millions of us see these men in ways that never were possible from the stands and impossible to convey through print. Like many others, I began watching as a student, then as a kind of participant. If the announcers sometimes lapsed into incomprehensible jargon, the best of them helped explain the subtleties of a game that I never had played.

The development of television technology was another important factor. Tight close-ups, instant replays, slow-motion cameras, even those incessant diagrams (used as if the announcers were explaining the Battle of Waterloo) helped make it possible to experience the ferocity of the game while understanding its redeeming qualities of grace and intelligence. I wasn't alone, of course. Pro football became a dominating American sport only after the triumph of television.

Now the game is part of my year. I root for the local teams, most of the time. As a Brooklyn Dodgers baseball fan, I grew up with the awful burden of explaining why, until 1955, the Dodgers, the greatest team in America, always lost the World Series. So I root for the Buffalo Bills, too. Most of all, I root for Joe Montana. It doesn't matter for what team he plays. Year after year, in game after game, on good days and bad, in victory and defeat, he has been an ornament of his time.

There is no vulgar showboating in Montana. There is no cheap con man's hustle. There is no tinhorn narcissism. Every time we see Montana work, we witness the cool, tough economy of the true professional. And more. There is pride without vanity. There is intelligence without self-delusion. There is a soldier's sense of integrity of the unit. Above all, Montana brings to the playing field the creativity of the artist. He seems to have done everything. But he always takes the field as if he can do even more, as if he still can examine a problem and conjure a surprise.

In combat, you would follow Montana against the best-defended outpost. Even if he was wrapped in bloody bandages, somehow he'd find a way to battle to the top of the ridge. He's a superb athlete, but he's more than that, just as football is more than a game.

There is much to learn on those hard striped fields, and it's not all about rollouts, pass patterns, and sacks. Look at Montana. Even for those who are no longer young, he has much to teach.

JIMMY CARTER

A FRIENDLY TAP

The formula for success on the
playing field is the same as the
formula for success in life

FROM SUPER BOWL XXVIII

AMERICANS LONG HAVE HAD A LOVE AFFAIR with sports. For generations, athletes have dominated the popular culture and served as role models for the young.

In my early years, I followed the triumphs of Red Grange and Joe DiMaggio. Later we thrilled to the feats of Joe Montana and Hank Aaron, but the feelings are the same.

We dream of doing what stars do—catching the impossible pass, besting the unbeatable foe, scoring the game-winning touchdown. We want to be like our heroes, both on the field and off.

What is it that makes athletes so inspiring? A true star builds a reputation not on the strengths of one game, but on a career shaped by talent, hard work, discipline, and dedication to the game.

And there is another important ingredient to success both on and off the athletic field: teamwork.

A football player cannot reach the Super Bowl alone, no matter how talented he is or how hard he works.

He must learn to trust his teammates, he must rely on them. Which means he must ignore the color of his teammate's skin, the place where he grew up, or the house of worship in which he prays.

This formula for success on the playing field is the same as the formula for success in life. All of us can develop the traits of champions in our own lives, whether our ambitions lie in the sporting arena, in the classroom, in the boardroom, or even in the White House.

Sports played an important role in my life when I was growing up in the small, rural town of Plains, Georgia. I played varsity baseball and basketball in high school, and ran cross-country at Annapolis. I also played football there—but in the under-140 pounds league! I never was a superstar, nor did I expect to play on a professional team.

But I enjoyed testing myself against others and against my own expectations. I learned firsthand about the importance of perseverance and teamwork.

Unfortunately, too many young children today are missing out on the important contributions sports can make to their lives.

There is a desperate need in our country for meaningful youth activities on weekends and after school, especially in troubled neighborhoods. Young people need adult role models and mentors to give them constructive alternatives to the destructive lifestyles many find all too easily on the street.

Schools, churches and synagogues, Boys' and Girls' Clubs, YMCAs, YWCAs, parks and recreation departments, and many other groups organize youth sports leagues and teams in their communities, but many of them never reach our inner cities, and they cannot make those efforts successful without active public support. They need coaches, jerseys, equipment, and space in which to play, and these are things that only we, as parents and neighbors and friends, can provide.

Our children need not just helmets and hoops but us—our car-ing, our commitment, and our time. They need dedicated people to bring their heroes' ideals home to them and help them learn the many lessons that team and individual sports can provide.

I know what that kind of personal involvement can mean because I have seen its impact in Atlanta.

Nearly a decade ago, we at The Carter Center launched The Atlanta Project (TAP) to tackle some of the many social problems that are tearing apart families and communities in the inner city—instability in the home, teenage pregnancy, unemployment, violence and drug abuse, and inadequate health care, among others.

TAP is designed to channel Atlanta's talent and goodwill into a coordinated effort to restore hope to the lives of people who have struggled for too long without it.

We work on the simple premise that people do not respond to programs; they respond to people.

TAP helps communities organize under the leadership of neighbors and friends. In partnership with thousands of volunteers and with government, other nonprofit organizations, and local businesses and universities, we are giving people the tools they need to identify their own problems and create their own solutions.

Let me give you an example of how TAP works. A few years ago, TAP launched the most comprehensive immunization campaign ever undertaken in this country. During one weekend, 12,000 volunteers went door-to-door to tell parents in inner-city neighborhoods about the importance of childhood immunizations. Thanks to their efforts, more than 16,000 preschoolers visited area health clinics in just one week.

We continue to work with local health departments, locating children and computerizing their health records to ensure that they receive adequate follow-up health care services.

Good physical health is one ingredient a child needs to develop his or her full potential, but there are other needs. That's why residents of the 20 neighborhoods TAP covers are involved in more than 250 community-based programs of their own, ranging from school mentoring programs to art and theater projects.

A number of programs involve Atlanta's sports community.

A group called Soccer in the Streets is working with a number of TAP communities to teach soccer to young people. Several members of the Atlanta Hawks helped restore homes around the city last summer, and members of the Atlanta Falcons and other local sports teams helped publicize TAP's very successful "Pennies From Heaven" fund-raising drive last fall.

As part of my work with TAP, I have spent many hours visiting with and listening to residents in some of the most disadvantaged communities in and around Atlanta. What I heard at some of those first meetings surprised me.

When we asked residents what were the most pressing needs in their neighborhoods, they consistently cited recreational facilities, after-school and weekend sports programs, and summer activities for kids. In fact, they listed this concern above the need for additional police protection and other much-needed social services.

TAP is responding to the residents' call by continuing to develop grassroots partnerships with the sports community. TAP clusters also are joining forces with our city's Boys' and Girls' Clubs, YMCAs, and Police Athletic Leagues.

Children have benefited tremendously from the NFL's own Youth Education Town. Because sports transcend racial, ethnic, and socioeconomic barriers, we believe the spirit of camaraderie and understanding among people can spill over into their everyday lives.

I hope you will explore how you can introduce opportunities for organized sports into your communities, not just for your own kids, but for your neighbors' children and those throughout your city.

Find out which programs need your help. In communities where programs do not yet exist, recruit a local business to sponsor a team. You'll be giving kids positive role models and helping them explore their own potential for excellence.

SCOTT OSTLER

ALL CHIN, ALL GLARE

In a lifetime of coaching, Don Shula
learned to adjust, but he never learned to
accept anything less than the best

FROM SUPER BOWL XXIX

B IOLOGISTS SPECULATE that in the event of an all-out nuclear war, cockroaches will be the earth's only survivors, which means Miami still would have an active night life.

But Bubba Smith, former all-pro defensive end, has his own theory.

"If a nuclear bomb were to be dropped," Smith says, "the only two things I'd bet would survive would be AstroTurf and Don Shula."

In Miami, the smart cockroaches have their money on Shula, because AstroTurf is subject to burnout.

Shula, coach of the Miami Dolphins, does not burn out. He simmers and cooks, stews and boils over, but he wins and wins.

He has 337 victories in 32 years as a head coach in the NFL—73 in seven seasons with the Baltimore Colts and 264 in 25 seasons with the Dolphins. He passed the late George Halas (324) in 1993 and didn't even slow down to beep his horn and wave.

Now Shula is 65, and the rumors and whispers are true: The game has passed him by. Fortunately for the Dolphins, the game that has passed him by is golf, which refuses to be intimidated by Shula. But football pass Don Shula by? No way. Football is frantically chasing Shula, who sprints toward paydirt, carrying with him the secrets of success that began in the days of Elvis.

"If you try to figure out Shula," Bubba Smith says, "he'll go the opposite way, just to remain a mystery to you. Shula's a beautiful piece of work, man."

He is a piece of work chiseled out of small-town Ohio granite, forged like steel in Cleveland, toughened up in waterfront Baltimore, and hard-baked under three decades of Miami sunshine.

Not everyone would agree that Shula is beautiful, and he never has been voted Mr. Congeniality. But his scorecard boggles the mind.

Halas coached until he was 73 and when Shula is asked if he can see himself coaching at 73, he shrugs and says, "As long as I enjoy it and we're doing well, I can't think of anything else I'd rather be doing."

This is great news in south Florida, where Shula is no mere legend. He is a living shrine, the state's most recognizable landmark, Miami's one-guy Mt. Rushmore.

Shula is so big in Miami—-and in football—that he can't be discussed as a whole. You have to break him down into his component parts, the pieces of the piece of work. The *piéce de résistance* of coaches.

THE GLARE
"The Glare?" Shula says in mock surprise, when asked about the look which freezes coffee and players' hearts.

"It's a nice, friendly smile."

It is none of the three. It is Shula's wrath on a laser beam. It contains elements of confrontation, intimidation, humiliation, and scorn. It elminates a lot of guesswork.

"I let my emotions out," Shula says. "I don't mask 'em, I just let 'em go. People can read me very easily. It's part of my personality, I don't spend time trying to figure out how to manipulate. I think any time you have to do anything that's contrived, the players sense it and it's not very effective."

Players go to great lengths to be spared the Glare. How can we sugar-coat this Shula bluntness? Give it a try, Bubba Smith.

"Shula was a thug," Smith says. "He was tough, he had a drive to win, and if you didn't have that same drive, he didn't deal with you."

"He scared the crap out of me," says Jim Mandich, who was the Dolphins' top draft pick in Shula's first Miami season, and lasted eight seasons. "He had me off balance right from the beginning. I came to camp driving a '62 Valiant with flowers painted all over it. I was wearing bell-bottoms, a tank top, sandals, love beads, and had long hair.

"I walked into Shula's office. He took one glance and said, 'You're *Mandich*? You *were the captain of the Michigan football team*?'"

Shula had great hang time on the word "you."

Any friendliness a player gets from Shula is hard-earned.

"My rookie year I made a lot of mistakes," says Jim Jensen, a college quarterback who played his way onto the Dolphins as a special-teams hit man. "He'd say things—just about have me in tears. I was at the point I almost felt like quitting. It's embarrassing. He calls you names, every name in the book."

And yet, Jensen lasted 12 seasons under Shula. Now Jensen plays arena football and often finds himself using Shula mannerisms and expressions. In difficult life situations, Jensen often asks himself, "What would Shula do here?"

Shula is the headmaster of a reverse finishing school. Instead of smoothing out the rough edges, he roughs up the smooth ones.

"I needed a pretty stern message delivered," Mandich says. "I needed to be told, 'You're really stepping up in class. It's gonna take a lot more effort and commitment than you thought it would take to play in the NFL.' Shula got the best player out of Jim

Mandich he could get, and that's the essence of coaching."

Shula develops friendships with some of his players, but only after they retire.

"Evervone was talking about the Jets early this season," Mandich says. "About how [coach] Pete Carroll was having pizza parties for the team, and isn't this great and fun? I thought, 'Man, you don't have a clue. The players are not your buddies.' You need a hell of a lot of meanness in you to coach in the NFL."

The only Dolphins who really kidded around with Shula were on the Larry Csonka-Jim Kiick-Mercury Morris team that went 17-0 in 1972, the only perfect season in NFL history. Csonka and Kiick once turned loose a live alligator in Shula's shower. Everyone (except the alligator) had a good laugh, and maybe the lesson was: You can joke around with the coach as long as you win every week.

THE JAW

The Shula Jaw is functional. It is shaped like the cowcatcher on an old locomotive, and it pushes aside life's debris, clearing the track for the Shula Express. The Jaw sweeps away critics, whiners, slackers, bluffers, glad-handers, chit-chatters, time-wasters, psycheprobers, and an occasional movie star.

Shula has been introduced to Kevin Costner and to Don Johnson, and he didn't have the faintest idea who either man was.

One Sunday a team official forgot to inform Shula that a certain author had been granted front-office permission to sit in on the Dolphins' halftime meeting, to do book research. Shula saw a stranger with a pad and pen and became livid.

"Who the hell is that sunovabitch?" Shula thundered.

"A writer," he was told.

"Get him the hell out of here!"

James Michener, meet Don Shula.

He is a man of routine, a creature of habit. He keeps his appointment with God each morning at early Mass, and then the world goes on Shula time.

"Nothing in the routine has changed one bit in the ten years I've been here," says Jeff Dellenbach, offensive lineman. "It's a running joke. Someone will ask, 'Why do we do [a certain drill] this way? And someone else will say, 'Because that's the way they did it in '72.'"

And yet it would be wrong to categorize Shula as inflexible. In judging attitudes, he differentiates between players who are harmful to the team, and players who are a thorn in his own side but can get the job done. The former go; the latter stay.

Bubba Smith, who was a Colts' rookie in Shula's fifth season in Baltimore, didn't break into the starting lineup until after he copped an attitude and got in Shula's face.

"My first year, I was Joe College, Peter Prep," Smith says. "He had me at tackle, and my legs were too long to play there, so most of the time I was on the bench. He was so strong-willed, he wasn't going to move me to end.

"My second year, I came back and really challenged Shula. I came to camp looking like Rap Brown—big Afro and love beads. The sportswriters said, 'Is Shula going to make you cut your hair?' I said, 'Is he my barber or my coach?'"

It was a daily glare-off at 20 paces, but Bubba could play, so Shula moved him to end and Smith became a star. Not long after that, Shula was one of the first coaches to stock the team shower room with black hair-care products.

"The fact that my wife and I raised five kids helped me as a coach to understand the changing problems of young people," Shula says. "When Dave was nineteen, Mike was thirteen. We had five teenagers at once. I had to learn how to deal with their problems. That helped me deal with young players."

Shula surrounds himself with crackerjack assistants—nine have gone on to NFL head coaching jobs—and stays ahead of the curve. In the old days, Shula was offensively conservative, even when he had Johnny Unitas at quarterback. Now Dolphins' quarterback Dan Marino usually passes more often than anyone in football.

"The great thing about Shula is the way he's adjusted," says Hank Stram, former Kansas City coach. "Not many of us ever had his sort of flexibility."

SCOTT OSTLER

Whatever the challenge—a player, the culture, the game—Shula handles it the same way. He points his chin down the track and shovels the coal.

"You've got to have the courage of your convictions," Shula says. "Mentally, physically, morally, you've got to have the courage. Somehow, some way, you've got to get the job done."

THE HEART

It was the summer of 1958. Don and Dorothy Shula were on their honeymoon at Ocean City, New Jersey. They were strolling along the seashore when Don stopped and asked Dorothy to backpedal. You know, run backwards in the sand.

"Why?" she asked, appropriately.

"I want to see how agile you are," he explained. "Football players have to be agile, and I want to see if our offspring have a chance to be players."

Don wasn't kidding. So Dorothy backpedaled. Shula's critics use this story to illustrate Shula's coldness, but actually it shows the opposite. Young Don was so smitten with love that he committed a major coaching blunder. He should have conducted the agility test before proposing. What if Dorothy had been clumsy?

"I would've been stuck," Shula says with a smile.

He smiles often when he talks about Dorothy, whom he met in a bowling alley in their hometown of Painesville, Ohio. They were a mutual admiration and inspiration society for more than 32 years. They had five children, and the two boys inherited enough backpedaling dexterity to become NFL players.

Dorothy died of breast cancer in 1991, after a terrible four-year illness. The first time Don Shula's kids ever saw him cry was at her funeral.

He was devastated. For weeks he wandered around their home, feeling Dorothy's presence, sinking in despair and loneliness.

What saved Shula was his family. He had always had a coach-player relationship with his kids, but with Dorothy gone, he knew he had to do what she had begged him to do—let down the emotional walls.

"He was never the kind of father who could tell you he loved you, who would hold you or kiss you," says Donna, the oldest Shula daughter. "It was real awkward for him. It's funny some of the things that you can talk to him about, things like your personal relationships, things you would never dream of telling him before. He tells us he loves us a lot more, too."

Nearly a year after Dorothy's death, Shula went to a New Year's party and met Mary Anne Stephens, a wealthy political and philanthropic activist. Two months later he worked up the courage to ask her for a date, and a year and a half later, they married.

A new Shula has emerged, wearing flowered shirts and designer clothes, snorkeling in the ocean, going to tennis camp in California. Opening up more, even with his players.

"I definitely think he's changed," recently retired linebacker John Offerdahl says. "He enjoys football maybe a little more. I see him smile a little more. When I first came, everything was business, business, business. Now he finds time to slide in a joke, loosen it up a little."

Not that Shula hasn't always had a soft, sentimental side. He still thinks of that day on the beach with Dorothy, and he smiles.

"Quick feet," he says.

THE BELLY

Due south of the Chin is the Shula Belly. It is well known for its stubborn refusal to shrink, despite Shula's relentless jogging and dieting. But the Belly is even more famous as home office of the Shula Fire.

"I was born with it," Shula says, referring to the fire, not the belly.

He was raised in little Painesville, Ohio, and was the boss of the local playground, even though he was the smallest and youngest kid in the neighborhood.

When his sixth grade football team lost, Shula ran under the stands and sobbed. In high school and in college, his teammates called him "coach," and it was not always a term of endearment.

"More than once," he says, "I was told in plain terms, 'Hey, you worry about yours and I'll worry about mine.'"

He was a hard-nosed running back at little John Carroll University, then he faced a career decision.

"I had a teaching minor in math," Shula says, "and I wanted to coach and teach in high school. When I graduated from college, I had a job offer in Canton, Ohio, at Lincoln High School, for $3,700. I was drafted by the Browns and they offered me a contract for $5,000. I decided to shoot for the moon."

He was simply taking a more roundabout route to Canton, now home of the Pro Football Hall of Fame. He played five seasons at defensive back for the Browns and Colts, then went into coaching as an assistant at Virginia. Five seasons and two jobs later, he was hired as head coach of the Baltimore Colts at age 33.

Shula is so driven that he had missed only one full day of work in 32 seasons, and that was because of Dorothy's illness, until he suffered a ruptured Achilles tendon just last December and underwent surgery. Still, he did not miss the next game, riding the sideline in a golf cart. And coaching. His energy is legendary. He does the work of two men—coach and general manager.

Burnout? Shula is more likely to be stricken by beriberi. Burnout is for guys whose supply of football passion is exhaustible.

On the sideline on Sundays, Shula is a maniac, all chin and glare and bark, the fire seemingly raging out of control. Yet he runs the ship with a steady hand, and later has uncanny recall of every play.

"I don't know that I'll ever find a substitute for what happens on game day, when the ball is kicked off," Shula says. "The emotional roller coaster. When I lose that, I'll know it's time to look for something else. I haven't lost that."

THE RECORD

Some perspective on Shula's career victory total: The active NFL coach closest to Shula is Chuck Knox with 193 wins. If Shula never wins another game and Knox averages 10 wins a year, he will catch Shula in the year 2009, at the age of 77.

Shula's lifetime winning percentage is fourth on the all-time

NFL list of coaches with 100 or more victories, behind John Madden (.731), George Allen (.681), and Joe Gibbs (.683). But those three coaches had a combined total of 34 NFL seasons.

Shula is too busy coaching to wallow in his numbers and records, but he is aware of whom he passed to become football's winningest coach.

"To me," he says, "the two most important people in the NFL were George Halas and Paul Brown."

Shula played under Brown in Cleveland, then coached under Brown disciple Blanton Collier at the University of Kentucky. Shula also coached under George Wilson, a Halas disciple, and then, as a head coach, went head-to-head with Halas. In their nine meetings, Colts vs. Bears, Shula came out with a 5-4 edge.

"Their two styles were in direct contrast, and I learned from both," Shula says. "From Halas I learned the handling of men and the toughness and competitiveness of the game. From Paul I got the teacher-pupil relationship. Paul put the classroom into pro football."

THE EMPIRE

Just northwest of Miami is the town of Miami Lakes, which really should be named Shulaville. Bearing the name and signature of Don Shula are two hotels, a steak house, a sports bar/restaurant, an executive golf course, and a huge athletic club.

You can shop from a full line of Don Shula golf clothing, and everything from golf balls to hotel soap to match books is stamped with a drawing of the famed Shula profile.

At the plush Don Shula Steak House, the menu is inscribed on a real football. The biggest cut is a 48-ounce porterhouse, bigger than your menu, and if you eat the entire steak, your name is engraved on a small gold plaque and bolted to the wall. Management assumes no responsibility for any fire that might start in your belly.

That 48-ounce club is the perfect Shula touch: To be rewarded, you must push yourself beyond sane limitations, eliminate all distractions, dig in, and go to work.

No excuses. Somehow, some way, you've got to get the job done.

WILL McDONOUGH

GATE-CRASHERS
AND FROGS' LEGS

There isn't enough room in a reporter's
notebook for all the indelible memories
that the Super Bowl has generated

FROM SUPER BOWL XXVIII

THE ASSIGNMENT was to cover the Kansas City Chiefs as they prepared to play the Green Bay Packers in Super Bowl I. Get out there a few days early, my boss at the *Boston Globe* told me, and stay at the same hotel as the Chiefs. Unheard of today, a reporter rooming at the same place as a Super Bowl team. But that's how it was in 1967.

I drove from the Los Angeles airport to Long Beach. It was dark, it was raining, and fog engulfed the hotel. The scene was like something out of the movies. It was a fitting introduction to this event, because the whole idea of the game was shrouded in mystery. One opinion seemed universal, however—the contest figured to be a mismatch.

Now, while sometimes things are what they appear (Super Bowl I *was* a mismatch, with Green Bay dominating), there are times when even the most vivid imagination cannot see what lies ahead.

Hard feelings ran deep in those days. NFL players and even the writers who covered them seemed indignant at the mere thought of having to play an AFL team. Len Dawson, the great Kansas City quarterback, was sitting at a coffee shop one morning when a writer from Cleveland approached. "Lenny," said the NFL writer, "I'd like to talk to you for a few minutes." Dawson, who had played with the Browns, shook his head. "Why? You never talked to me the years I was in Cleveland."

Access to players never was a problem then. That's a far cry from today, when you almost need an act of Congress to get an interview, then have to battle MTV reporters to ask a question.

A few days before the first Super Bowl, I drove up to Santa Barbara, where the Packers were staying. I asked to see quarterback Bart Starr. Next thing I knew, Starr appeared in the hotel lobby and told me to come to his room.

Interview a player in his hotel room before the Super Bowl? Not a chance of doing that today.

I felt bad for the Chiefs that Sunday. My heart was with them, as were the hearts of most of the AFL writers. It was a personal thing with us. The late Tex Maule of *Sports Illustrated* basked in the spotlight. He was an NFL guy, and he told anyone who would listen that Green Bay would dominate.

He was right. The AFL writers had to bite their tongues.

The bashing continued in the locker room. Legendary Vince Lombardi was asked about the Chiefs. "Well," said the Packers head coach, "they can't play with the good teams in our league. They couldn't play with the Lions or Bears [Green Bay's chief rivals in the NFL Western Conference]."

After filing my story, I went back to the hotel and sat around a small press room with Kansas City head coach Hank Stram and a few AFL writers. Stram, told of Lombardi's comments, was devastated. He talked about the game, but every couple of minutes he'd say, "Did Vince *really* say we weren't that good? That we couldn't play at that level? Vince is a friend. Did he *really* say that?"

That summer, returning to the *Boston Globe* after a Red Sox game, I passed the wire machine and saw that Kansas City had defeated Chicago 66-24 in a preseason game. I said to myself: "I'm sure that was for you, Vince."

But even Lombardi came around. The day before Super Bowl III in January, 1969, I was with Jimmy Cannon, the late and very great New York columnist and a friend of Lombardi's. "Kid," Cannon told me, "I think they [the Jets] have a shot."

I laughed. Hell, the Jets were 19-point underdogs. It was just a hopeful New Yorker talking, I thought. "No, I was talking to Vince," Cannon said, "and he thinks this kid [Joe Namath] can beat them. They're better than they used to be."

In more than 30 years of sportswriting, that game remains my biggest thrill. Namath was masterful, but I'll always remember hearing of coach Weeb Ewbank's pregame speech. "*When* we win," he told his players, "don't carry me off the field. I have a bad hip. I don't want to get hurt."

His players thought it was a ploy to show how confident he was. But Ewbank was serious. In the AFL Championship Game two weeks earlier, he was carried off the field and a fan had pulled so hard on his leg that he required hip surgery later that year.

If Super Bowl III was vindication for the AFL, it also was sweet justice for the writers from the junior league. Maule got an earful from us. *The tables had turned.*

Respect grew the next year when Stram, Dawson, and the Chiefs beat the NFL's mighty Vikings at Tulane Stadium. It was the most bizarre Super Bowl week ever. It was abnormally cold in New Orleans, the Mississippi River was frozen, rumors circulated that Dawson was involved in gambling, and nobody seemed convinced that the Jets' victory the year before was real. I truly believed the Chiefs would win, but they were huge underdogs.

This was the game in which a hot-air balloon crashed into the stands during halftime. Fortunately, many of the fans were huddling under the stands to escape the cold, so no one was badly hurt.

Which is more than I could say for myself. Sick with the flu, I decided to eat something solid for the first time in days. I opened my box lunch, had a few bites, turned to a Cleveland writer, Chuck Heaton, and told him the chicken was pretty good, "That's not chicken," he said, "it's frogs' legs." I think I could have outrun Otis Taylor in my sprint to the men's room.

Super Bowl history books tell us all about the great plays and the players who pulled them off. My favorite Super Bowl memories are drawn not from people who performed between the goal posts, but from those who added flavor and human qualities.

People such as Skipper McNally. Skipper was a character, a guy from the Boston area who'd had bit parts in some good movies such as *Charly* and *On the Waterfront*. Skipper was a gate-crasher; he loved the spotlight, and what brighter spotlight than America's premier sporting event? In New Orleans for Super Bowl IV, he devised a scheme. When the team bus approached Tulane Stadium, Skipper put on his Vikings windbreaker and yelled out: "Team's here. Clear the way. Team's here." He ran beside the bus as it went through the gates and past security.

When it became apparent the Chiefs would win, Skipper changed gears. He put on a Kansas City windbreaker and moved to the other sideline. His goal was to help carry off the winning coach, to get his picture in *Sports Illustrated*. So as time ran out, there was 5-foot-9 Skipper McNally next to 6-foot-9 Ernie Ladd, the former Chief who was cheering on his ex-mates.

"Grab the coach," said Ladd. Skipper obliged. He made his *SI* photo and also the NFL highlight reels because NFL Films had wired Stram. On the film, you can hear Stram calling out: "Where's Grant [Vikings head coach Bud Grant], where's Grant?"

Skipper was tired and sore, in no mood to carry Stram any longer. "Coach," you can hear him say on the tape, "*bleep* Grant. Let's get out of here."

In 1977, a great guy who had suffered terrible disappointments on the football field, Raiders head coach John Madden, got to taste Super Bowl success. That day in Los Angeles didn't start well for Madden. A bundle of nerves, he was in such a rush to head to the Rose Bowl that he left four players at the hotel.

He fined himself for making them late. Later, after a 32-14 rout of the Vikings, Madden celebrated by shaking hands with folks in the parking lot, then retiring to a trailer with his boyhood friend, USC coach John Robinson. Madden still is the same unpretentious man today.

At Super Bowl XVI, San Francisco head coach Bill Walsh got to Detroit earlier than his team. He had gone somewhere to pick up an award, so he decided to meet the players when they arrived at the hotel in Detroit. Dressed in a bellhop's uniform, Walsh greeted the 49ers and kidded with them, telling them they were going to get their butts kicked. Several players absorbed the abuse before Walsh was recognized.

When Super Bowl XXI came to Los Angeles, I was doing some television work for CBS, and it was a new experience. It's a major production, but much of it is done on the fly. My pregame interview from the field was going to be with Denver owner Pat Bowlen, but at the last second my producer nixed the idea. "Do something else," he said.

So we opted for a quick piece on stadium security. I positioned myself near the Giants bench and immediately got smacked a few times by a woman with a baton. I was standing where the band needed to line up, she yelled.

Stay there, said my producer, even if it meant getting hit. Which it did. The security piece included something about gate-crashers (I would have loved to tell the story of Skipper) and a skydiver who had warned that he was going to parachute in during the National Anthem. He never did. Who knows, maybe he decided to wait for a heavyweight championship fight seven years later.

Later, we headed to the losers' locker room for interviews. An NFL official was furious because we got there before the Broncos, so he made us hide in the showers. That's where we were when coach Dan Reeves talked to his players.

Moving toward the locker room just before halftime that day, I went past a group of people who were getting ready to entertain. A man dressed as a clown tapped me on the shoulder. "Hey, pal, I haven't been out there yet, who's winning the game?" I told him it was close, but the Giants were starting to play well. "Whew, good," he said. "I have a bet on the Giants." It was Mickey Rooney.

I've known Buffalo Bills owner Ralph Wilson since the old AFL days. His team lost to the Giants in Super Bowl XXV, remembered forever as the game in which Scott Norwood's 47-yard field goal attempt in the final seconds was wide right.

Two years later, Wilson invited me to the Kentucky Derby. He had a financial interest in the favorite, Arazi. I glanced at the *Racing Form* as we drove to Churchill Downs. "Ralph," I asked, "what number did Scott Norwood wear?" He thought for a moment and said, "Eleven." I showed him the Racing Form and pointed to horse number 11, Arazi.

The program said Arazi liked to run wide right. We laughed at the irony.

I don't know much about racing, so I tried to follow Arazi. I knew his jockey wore a red cap. Toward the stretch the horses bunched and I focused on the finish line. I thought I saw a jockey with a red cap finish first. I thought Arazi had won.

Wilson pulled back from his binoculars. He didn't say a word. He simply made a sweeping motion with his hands: wide right. I told Wilson I thought Arazi had won. (He hadn't.)

"Will, the day of the Super Bowl," Wilson said, "when Norwood kicked that ball, when the ball was in the air, I was up in the box. I jumped off the ground and said, 'We won!' But then it went wide right. So I won the Super Bowl for three seconds."

Three glorious seconds...27 memorable games. It's all a matter of perspective.

JIM THOMAS

ONCE UPON A TIME...

Five years after bagging groceries for
$5.50 an hour, Kurt Warner lived a dream
that took him to the Super Bowl

FROM SUPER BOWL XXXIV

KURT WARNER DIDN'T WALK OUT of an Iowa cornfield to take the NFL by storm. It only seems that way. Besides, in his field of dreams, the Rams' quarterback always pictured himself catching passes, not throwing them.

"I always wanted to be a receiver," Warner says. "I always was a receiver until I was in high school."

Because Regis High School in Cedar Rapids, Iowa, was desperate for a quarterback when Warner was a freshman, he reluctantly switched positions. The rest is, well, folk history.

In the feel-good story of the 1999 NFL season, this unlikeliest of candidates for stardom emerged from the bottom of the Rams' depth chart to become a pro football Cinderella. Just five years earlier, he had been bagging groceries for $5.50 an hour at the Hy-Vee Supermarket in Waterloo, Iowa, where he told anyone who would listen that someday he'd play in the NFL.

Sure, kid, now get down to register three and help that old lady out to her car.

Talk about pedigrees. Or the lack of same. Warner didn't get a single NCAA Division I-A scholarship offer. He didn't start until his senior season at I-AA Northern Iowa. His first NFL tryout, with Green Bay in 1994, ended almost before it began when he found himself on a depth chart that also included Brett Favre, Mark Brunell, and Ty Detmer. Warner didn't get another NFL try-out until the Rams came calling nearly four years later.

Even that invitation was something less than open-armed. That the Rams expressed an interest at all can be traced to the dogged persistence of Al Luginbill, coach of the Amsterdam Admirals in the NFL Europe League.

Luginbill had heard of Warner's passing prowess for the Iowa Barnstormers of the Arena Football League (he passed for 183 touchdowns in three seasons), but the coach could acquire the quarterback for his team only if an NFL club tendered Warner a contract and assigned him to the Amsterdam team. Ten or so NFL teams listened patiently to Luginbill and rebuffed his sales pitch before the Rams and the Chicago Bears indicated mild interest.

When an elbow injury kept Warner from trying out for the Bears on the day they had set aside, they backed off. Later, in what could have been his last opportunity, the Rams gave Warner a look and saw enough to sign him to a contract.

"Two things caught your eye at the workout," says Charley Armey, the Rams' vice president of player personnel. "Number one, he was extremely accurate. He never made the receivers work to catch the ball. In this business, arm strength is so overrated, and accuracy is underrated. Number two, he got rid of the ball so quick."

Warner's talent seems patently obvious now after a season in which he ranked among the league's leading quarterbacks and led St. Louis to the NFC West title.

But, oh, so many puzzle pieces had to fall in place.

After leading NFL Europe in passing yards and touchdowns in

the spring of 1998, and being the Rams' number-three quarterback during the 1998 season, Warner was rewarded by the Rams last summer when he was elevated to the number-two quarterback spot behind Trent Green, a $16.5 million free-agent pickup from the Washington Redskins. But it was a tenuous promotion at best. Warner was exposed—and went unclaimed—in the expansion draft that stocked the Cleveland Browns. Then, before training camp, Rams coach Dick Vermeil debated whether to bring in a veteran to battle for the backup role. Talk about having to earn respect.

"The man obviously didn't take the elevator to get here," Carolina Panthers linebacker Kevin Greene says. "He took the stairs. And he started at the very freakin' bottom of the staircase. Then they put him in the basement, and he still came back up. So you've got to say, 'Hats off to the guy.'"

Warner humbly accepts all the praise. But he's not surprised by his success.

"There were some doubts that I would get a chance," he says. "But there was never a doubt that I could come to this level and compete and be successful. Not in my mind, anyway.

"When you see all the steps along the way that helped me get to this point, well...it wouldn't be how I'd write my own script. But it's exactly what I needed to get me to the point where I am now, both as a person and as a player. That's what my faith does. It gives me the perspective to know that there's a reason why everything happens."

A strongly religious man, Warner's faith and family have kept him grounded. He keeps a photo of his family taped inside his locker as a constant reminder of what's important in his life. Perhaps that's why he never seems flustered on a football field.

"Whether I'm on the field or off the field, I don't get anxious," he says. "I don't get nervous. I don't get uptight. Because I know that things are going to work out for me. Through faith, and the things that happened in my family, I've learned how to react to those types of situations. I've learned that there's going to be speed bumps along the way, that it's not just going to be a smooth path."

Nothing has come easy for Warner, or for his wife Brenda. Warner's mother-in-law and father-in-law were killed in an Arkansas tornado in 1996. Brenda's son by a previous marriage, Zachary, suffered severe brain damage 10 years ago after being dropped on his head in a bath-time accident. Zach, whose life was in jeopardy, survived but is legally blind.

"He was completely blind when I took him home from the hospital," Brenda says. "Basically, the doctors told me to make the best of it. It was just difficult, obviously, but you just take it and make decisions that are best for the child."

Brenda's first husband never came to terms with the accident, and their marriage ended in divorce. Just before the birth of a daughter, Jesse, Brenda returned home to Iowa to live with her parents and start over.

Then Warner walked into her life. In 1992, Brenda and her mother went line dancing at a country music club. That's where she met Warner, who had accompanied a friend to the club. The two hit it off almost immediately, but Brenda never thought she'd see Kurt again. She was four years older than he, and she already had two children, one of whom required special care.

A lot of men might have been scared off, but Warner is not most men. He called on her the next day, a rose in his hand. After a five-year courtship, they married, and Warner adopted her children. Since then, they have added to the family with the birth of a son, Kade.

"I've been blessed with these kids," Warner says. "It's neat to see them mixed together. They're just incredible kids with all the talents and gifts they have on different spectrums. I have learned from them."

One year after meeting Brenda, Warner got his first start for Northern Iowa. And barely in time. He had given thought to transferring to another school.

"I was struggling with my situation," he says. "I felt I should be playing. I did not think I was getting the opportunity that I deserved."

Playing full time as a senior, Warner performed well enough to get his short-lived training-camp shot with Green Bay in 1994.

A job in the Arena Football League, from 1995-97, allowed Warner to stay in the game, sharpen his skills, and earn a few bucks. When he passed for 93 touchdowns in the 1997 season, it also gave him a chance to attract Luginbill's attention.

Almost immediately after signing with the Rams, Warner was assigned to NFL Europe. Playing on the "big field," as Warner called it, was an adjustment. But it was an easy adjustment. After playing for three seasons in the confined spaces of the Arena Football League, where every play unfolds at blinding speed, Warner said he had to slow down his game.

After starring for Amsterdam, Warner spent the 1998 NFL season in St. Louis behind Tony Banks and Steve Bono. He was slated for more of the same in 1999 before Green suffered a season-ending knee injury in preseason.

"When Trent Green went down, Dick never wavered," Armey says. "He went in and told Kurt, 'You're our quarterback.' And then he went in and told the players, 'We can win with this guy.'"

Then Warner went out, and, against all odds, proved his coach correct.

ROBERT JAMES WALLER

SIX MEN IN THE BIG EMPTY

Football games come in all sizes, the
novelist and former player explains, and big
doesn't necessarily equate to better

FROM SUPER BOWL XXX

OCTOBER COOL at sunrise, nine hours back. In the 80s now by midafternoon, and the high-desert light is incandescent even through frosted windows. Smell of sweat, old and new, in the cramped locker room.

Band playing out on the field. Fight song filtering through the walls, the melody made eternal by Notre Dame with the words tailored to fit us. Ready to make common cause, we have transformed from individuals into a single mind called team. We are a bowstring that has been pulled back day by day through the week just past, the bow now arched to its snapping point, until we have come to hate the very name of Fort Davis, to loathe the soul and essence of that pretty mountain town lying some 60 miles northeast of us.

Well, except for me. I'm having a little trouble generating hate, but in an effort to please the coach and be one of the team, I'm try-ing. I've been trying all week and working harder on it since I got up this morning. Actually, I'm thinking mostly about Francie, my month-old filly clawed by a mountain lion two days ago. Her right foreleg is chewed up pretty bad, but my dad nailed the lion with his old 30-30 about five seconds before Francie would have been buzzard meat. It was a heck of a shot, considering twilight and corral fences, not to mention the dust and excitement and all.

Silence for 10 minutes. We sit, heads down, forearms on knees and hands clenched. Someone goes to the water fountain, anoth-er to the toilet. Tension approaches agony—God, release this ar-row and let the Marathon Mustangs go forth to waste and ravage those pitiful Fort Davis Indians, those frauds who have the cheek and gall to label themselves football players.

The band rolls into its fourth iteration of the fight song. It's time. Coach claps his hands once. "Let's go." Scrape of cleats on the concrete floor, and the Marathon, Texas, six-man football team is launched into the pure light of a high desert afternoon.

Out comes Sammy Cavness. Comes next Jesus Estrada, our quarterback. After them, Jones and Aguilar. Then Garcia, Thomp-son...and the rest, all 10 of us. Including me, Delmore Rake, the last man out.

Okay, okay, I know you're saying, "Who?...Delmore Rake? What kind of a name is that?" Stop laughing, it's my name. In the way of the old Smucker's jam commercial, being saddled with a name like Delmore Rake means you've got to be good. Problem was, I wasn't. I didn't even like playing football. At 5 feet 2 inches and 97 pounds in my fourteenth year, plus having a bad case of slow, I didn't figure football was my game.

My dad didn't either. "Son, I believe the game is above yawl's bend, beyond your huckleberry, in a manner of speakin'. Along with the possibility of gettin' yawl's lamp blowed out, I've seen yawl run, and I don't believe yawl could catch a fat man with his britches down. Besides, we've got plenty to do here on the ranch without yawl draggin' in every day at seven o'clock, too tired to help."

But in Marathon, Texas, in 1965, if you weren't playing football, you didn't exist. The pressure was enormous to go out for the team, there being only 20 or so boys in the entire last four grades. So all hands and the cook were expected to rise when the call for players was issued. If you didn't, you were assigned names I can't repeat here, and you were more likely to be the object of physical beatings.

My dad, talking on and on about working cattle instead of lolly-gagging around a football field, wouldn't buy me proper shoes, so I had to practice in a pair of old sneakers. On game days, one of the junior high boys loaned me his high-tops with hard rubber cleats, the real thing. When everyone else had selected his equipment furnished by the school, I'd been left with pawing through salvage.

My thigh pads draped over my knees until the coach showed me how to tape them up, but they still jiggled a lot. Worse, the only shoulder pads among the leftovers were so big they lopped down to my elbows. My mother took several tucks in the number "49" jersey and cuffed the sleeves under so they didn't extend beyond my fingertips anymore. With my helmet in place, which had a way of resting on my shoulder pads and not sitting quite flat on my head, I had the appearance of some weird miniature robot from the old sci-fi comic books. Overall, and looking back, it was...well, pathetic.

But I was on the squad and in the program, which listed my number, age, height, weight, and grade in school: 49, Delmore Rake, 14, 5' 2", 97, Grade 9. The program also said I was a defensive back, though I wasn't sure what that meant when it came right down to it.

One of the seniors said I should be called Acorn, that being the name in those days for smaller folks, which he said would make me Acorn Rake on the program. The coach told the young man to hobble his lip and take three extra laps around the field at the conclusion of practice. Coach needed every warm body he could muster, including me, in my floppy thigh pads and sneakers.

This was the world of West Texas six-man football. Invented by one Mr. Stephen Epler in 1933 when he was short of players up in Chester, Nebraska. The game spread like mesquite across the far, dry land of the high desert, where the towns are small and the spaces huge. We practically had to travel the continent for our games. To make a night game at Fort Hancock over by El Paso, we loaded on a school bus at noon and arrived back home at 4 a.m.

Six-man football is a little different. Three backs, two ends, and a center. A slightly shorter and narrower field, and everybody's an eligible receiver. There's also the so-called mercy rule, where if one team gets up by 45 points, the game's finished. There's some other differences, too, but the overall result is a wide-open contest, the best elements of basketball and track stewed together with the normal blocking and tackling and passing. Scores such as 69-40 are common. If it sounds a bit ragtag, that'd be wrong. There's hard hitting and smart blocking in six-man, just as you find in the 11-man game. The players take it seriously. So do the small towns.

Not many who play six-man go on to college ball or the pros; the game has just enough dissimilarities with 11-man to make the transition difficult. And compared to the big-time football played in Odessa and Midland, it's hard to get noticed by scouts. Jack Pardee from Christoval and a couple others pulled it off, but that's all. Yet, watching two fine six-man teams go at it, you begin to think it's a great idea.

So Mustangs was our name and six-man was our game, and we were ready to play it on a Friday afternoon in Marathon. We hit the field, me picking up my stride as we passed the concession stand operated by the PTA. Lucinda Gonzales, who was also in ninth grade, was helping out in there, and I thought she was the prettiest thing I'd ever seen on earth, along with Francie, my filly.

The stands were packed. Around 200 people had paid a dollar each to see us take on Fort Davis. When the team played at home, Fridays were like a medieval festival in Marathon. People drove to the field early in the morning to secure a good place, backing their pickups almost onto the field and parking there. Later, they'd unfold lawn chairs and set them in the rear of the pickups.

Finally, the band got off the field, Sammy Cavness mumbling

something about them looking like Santy Ana's army in their uniforms. Vance Jones kicked off barefoot. Elias Dutchover tried to get it back upfield for Fort Davis, but fumbled. Sammy covered it, Manuel Garcia ripped off 18 yards for us, and Jones barreled over for a touchdown on the following snap. It went on that way. We pulled further ahead, and I started to fret I might get in the game and wondered what I'd do if I did. Not to worry; the coach knew better and left me alone by the cheerleaders and the water bucket.

I played three times that year. Once I went in as a running back, but Jesus Estrada gave the ball to Thompson who bolted 50 yards for a score, putting us up by 45, and the mercy rule was invoked. The second time, I became fascinated by a black-throated sparrow hopping around on the field. While I was admiring the sparrow's moxie, the other team threw a pass right by me for a touchdown.

I had one moment of glory, though it was the next thing to accidental. Balmorhea had this big halfback whose name I've forgotten, 220 pounds and fast, not to mention mean. Coach inserted me at defensive back only because two players were momentarily injured, and I'd drifted too near him while trying to get a better view of Lucinda in the concession stand. I stood out there terrified, hoping for a Balmorhea fumble or something. No luck. Handoff to the big hombre, around end and straight down the sideline he came, dusting trail with huge thighs pumping and looking like a berserk range bull headed for a touchdown. By instinct more than desire, I angled in his direction, all the while thinking, "Dad was right, Dad was right...." I was also thinking: "I hit him, I'm sausage."

But I caught my cleats in a gopher hole, stumbled, and fell in the bull's path. His right toe whacked into my hip pad, and he went down as if he'd been poleaxed. The coach called it a "gutsy play."

I gave up football after that year. My dad had a mild stroke, so everyone understood I had serious ranch work to do and left me alone. In time, I became a pretty decent bronco rider, which allowed me to wear big silver belt buckles I'd won in local rodeos. And somehow the name Delmore Rake sounded different coming out of the chute than it did coming out of the locker room.

The team on which I played for a season laid some track, though. In the late '60s and early '70s, under three different coaches, Marathon made five consecutive trips to the Texas six-man championships and won two of them. In 1976, short of six-man teams to play, the coach scheduled eight games against 11-man teams, all on the road because the home field couldn't be lengthened and widened. And Marathon won every one of them before reverting to six-man for the playoffs.

In the sum and total, what can be made of this? What did I bring away from the table that long freshman year in an ill-fitting uniform? Nothing I can lay my hands on.

Still, once every autumn when my wife is busy with something on a Friday night, Jack the border collie and I take the pickup and drive across the big empty of West Texas to whatever six-man game we can find.

I look over at Jack and say, "Mr. Pardee, it's a long way from here to the Super Bowl." But then I start thinking, everything's a long way from the Super Bowl.

Jack howls when the fans honk truck horns after an especially good play. Other than that, he and I grin at each other and eat popcorn, watching the game Stephen Epler invented 63 years ago, one of the best games that ever came to be. No dreams of the pros, none of that. Just some sweet passes, hard running, and lots of touchdowns. A game sized for small towns and small-town kids whose yellow school buses travel the big empty out here in search of someone to play.

WADDIE MITCHELL

THE GAME

Poet Waddie Mitchell pays tribute

in rhyming verse to the game

that demands—and gives back—so much

FROM SUPER BOWL XXX

FROM LATE SUMMER all through autumn
Into winter every year
Men and boys from town and country
Daily don their football gear.
And they run and sweat and swelter
Or they'll bounce to fight the chill
And they practice and they scrimmage
Working hard to hone their skill.
They pursue and dodge and fake out.
And they charge and turn and dive.
Thrust themselves at one another.
Dance a jig and slap high five.
Tape their fingers, wrists, and ankles.
Block the punt and study plays.

Dump big tubs of ice on coaches.
Hit the lockers in a daze.
They hand off, rush and sweep, and trip.
Fight jock itch.
Warm the bench.
Smear polish underneath their eyes.
Miss first downs by an inch.
They miss the tackle.
Miss a chance.
Might miss some Friday classes.
They miss not sleeping in a lot
And miss a lot of passes.
They're bruised and scraped and stepped on
But then right back up they jump.
They cuss the call. They huddle.
Pat each other on the rump.
Their fingers sting. They bellow steam
As moist air starts to freeze.
They flap caped wings and stomp their feet
To warm extremities.

They're gargantuan-looking monsters
   In their helmets and their pads
   Like the gene pools went awry
Between their mothers and their dads.
They call time out. They call a foul.
They call in their defense.
Call home to tell the folks they won.
Call overtime intense.
Call plays in from the sideline.
When it's close, call in the chain.
But it calls for a disaster
'Fore they'll ever call a game.
They learn the worth of teamwork
What it means to pull their weight
Earn respect and rings and letters

THE GAME

Learn to eat their supper late.
They tear ligaments and jerseys.
Plagued with fouls and injuries.
Make the catch and make up yardage.
Make mistakes and memories.
Make the news and interceptions.
Make the block that makes the hole.
Make a meat loaf for the pot luck.
Make it to the Super Bowl.
They adjust themselves in public!
Guzzle lots of Gatorade
And they go into hysterics
Every time a touchdown's made.
They use their intuition.
Use up all of their time outs.
They use a cup and mouthpiece
And they use recruiting scouts.
They use their cleats for traction
And their status on the team
To secure a date on prom night
With the school's homecoming queen.
Use their kicker to make field goals.
Go for the extra points.
Use strong-smelling rubbing balm
To loosen up sore joints.

They hike and spike and pile high
        Upon the frozen ground
        And they stop the clock from ticking
When the ball goes out of bounds.
They sack quarterbacks and fumble.
They stiff-arm, sneak, and blitz.
Shout encouragement to teammates.
Throw their helmets in a fit.
They go through camps and clinics
And they sometimes go through hell.

But think they've gone to heaven
If they reach the NFL.
Football's become synonymous
With special holidays
Like New Year's and Thanksgiving
Even Christmas nowadays.
It is as much American
As stories by Mark Twain.
As exciting as a rodeo.
As macho as John Wayne.
It is cheerleaders and glee clubs.
It is chess-like strategy.
It is comedy and drama.
It is floats and pageantry.
It's the Heisman Trophy winners.
Pros becoming household names.
It's the guys who coach Pop Warner.
It's the fans who go to games.
It's watched in bars and barber shops
In restaurants and at home.
It stirs up strong emotion
With a language of its own.
To some the game seems harsh
And often calls for sacrifice
But can teach a strong work ethic
And prepare one well for life.
It exercises traits we'll need
To help us to progress
And develops tools to work with
On our push towards success.
Like a staunch determination
And the will to never quit.
Like sportsmanship and fortitude
Commitment, pride, and grit.
And realizing that all people
On certain points are flawed,

THE GAME

In football we've a coach to lead
In life we have a God.
In both games we will get out
Nothing more than we put in.
We must accept those blows we take
If we expect to win.
But life's great lesson's there for us
To run with if we choose:
If we but give the best we've got,
We'll never really lose.

RICHARD FORD

JUST NOT GOOD ENOUGH

Novelist Richard Ford, author of The Sportswriter
and Independence Day, *learned one of life's most
important lessons on a football field*

FROM SUPER BOWL XXXII

MY ONLY TRUE—by which I mean hands-on—experience
in football took place in 1960, a long time ago now. It
was Mississippi. The genteel suburbs of Jackson. I was
16, fatherless. And for reasons I don't yet fully understand, toward
the end of my sophomore year in high school, and not long after
my father died, I elected to turn out for spring drills, even though
I'd never thought of playing football in my life.

Spring is a soft time in Mississippi. There are low, turbulent
clouds, winds growing blustery and cool. Often it rains. Great, un-
dulant streams of blackbirds begin to funnel toward the north. It
is a museful season, and so in no way a bad time to stand out on
a damp practice field in the afternoon, with people whom you
know, and to find out you are no good at something.

As elsewhere, then and now, football was sacramental at my

school. By playing it, even playing it terribly, a boy could reasonably expect to enjoy instant, pandemic social acceptance, be warmed by the illusions of maturity, savor success at a slightly too-early age, all of which allowed you to radiate physical prowess and oppressive self-confidence, and thus attract the attention of girls. Liberty, equality, fraternity this is sometimes expressed. I do not mean to make light of it. It was and is important.

The ways I was no good at football were not at all long revealing themselves. My height—a lanky 6-2—must have been what finally prompted me to "go out." I had a guilty suspicion I was too big not to play football; that, and my not particularly large but reasonably capable hands (I featured myself to be an end). Only I was slow, slow, slow afoot—last at everything requiring speed; so painfully slow as to be ignorant of even the concept of foot speed, and unable this day to understand how one person can actually run faster than another.

Beyond that, I remember how cumbersome and heavy the old gladiatorial equipment felt, and how ponderous and impaired I felt wearing it out on the windy practice ground. All the other would-be players, it seemed, carried their bodies somehow better than I did, with complete, thoughtless persuasiveness, whereas I was specious and unathletic, a lost cause ever to perform a graceful act. I remember how I hated skinning the much-too-tight helmet onto and off my head, how it scraped and gouged my scalp, and how, once in place, it seemed weighty and boulderish, and to require strict, self-conscious balancing more than to invite actual use as a hat. And I remember how I rattled when I ran, and how farfetched it seemed that my body ever could attain the sleek speed necessary to become an effective projectile. I moved, I'm sure, like a sick man moves, and like a sick man I was happiest when standing still.

And I hated the drills, all of them, but especially one where you and your paired-off buddy (mine was another aspiring end named Mike Simmons, who later starred), took three-point stances facing the other, then simply ran smack together. Head-on tackling this was called. And it hurt. I remember my shoulder whamming

flush-on into Mike Simmons's brick-like thigh, my head hopeful-
ly up, my hands gripped behind his big knees, my cleats digging
into the chewed-up turf, determined not to lose ground until the
whistle blew or one of us went over. And if it hurt to be tackled, it
hurt more, much more, to do the tackling, and I know for fact that
each time I charged Mike Simmons I did so with wilting ferocity,
hoping to inflict less pain on both of us.

And there was more. I could never budge the blocking sled, and
would sometimes simply stop blocking it altogether and stand and
stare at the strange, inert contraption as if it had a motor in it that
wouldn't work, all while the line coach, riding the other side, kept
shouting at me, "Come on, Ford, it won't hurt you. You're s'posed
to hurt it." And sometimes in the middle of drills or calisthenics
or sprints I would simply pause and look up at the quilted sky,
thinking who knows what. The wind would be gusting. Blackbirds
would be streaming high above. Someone might have been flying
a box kite far beyond the distant school buildings. (I cannot think
I had any picture of myself actually playing football. It wasn't fea-
sible.) Yet this is how it feels to be unmotivated. A feeling of serene
isolation. And though someone might say I was quizzical or curious, I was not curious about football.

But consequently all plays designed to sucker and deceive me
did. My football player's mentality became one of anticipating the
unknown with special loathing. And more than once I remember
standing in this very state of fearful abstraction while an actual
play was going forward; and while simply staring off, or possibly
even looking where I felt I should have been looking, I would be
flattened from my blind side by a hurtling halfback or his grunt-
ing blocker, and left in the muck.

My only even-remotely-near-real-life "action" came in a mean-
ingless intrasquad game, during which, on the very last play I reluctantly was sent in and told to perform a "button-hook" route. In
practice, this play had become "my" play over the spring weeks.
Indeed, it was the only one I could be relied on to perform with
even minimal uniformity. I simply had to run seven yards downfield, abruptly stop, turn (hook), face the quarterback, and receive

the ball (thrown before I hooked) more or less automatically while standing basically still (my favorite route), and then fall backwards (upfield) without turning loose of the ball—all of which I have, over the years, remembered performing flawlessly, after which the final gun sounded.

Yet sadly, my button-hook pass also is clouded by contingency and doubt—a function of age mingled with honest skepticism. I have only lately realized how brittly humiliating it was that this was "my" play, since it was "mine" only because it was so goofily simple. You didn't even have to be a football player to do a button-hook perfectly. And, even though countless times over the 37 years I've relived it—me accepting the softly thrown ball into my soft stomach, me clutching it with my two supposedly capable hands, me heaving breathlessly backwards for the crucial yard as the final seconds of the game and my brief career ticked down—I have now become uncertain if I actually did catch the ball, or if the pass was even thrown to me, or if I was the one sent in, or if such a game was played at all. John Updike wrote once that "...for the novelist, the halls of memory and imagination are adjacent spaces." And I am a novelist. And it is entirely possible that I have bestowed memorial gravity onto pure fantasy as a way of simply surviving football and my own inglorious experience of trying to play the game.

And if I did that, I forgive myself. Maybe being a terrible football player made me a better storyteller. Maybe this is what's meant by football being a "much-storied" game. Art, of course, often seeks residence in those vacant precincts of life where we have failed, retreated, remained untested, wondered but not dared.

My final memory is the quitter's memory—oddly sweet. I am walking up my suburban driveway, crushed by fatigue and irresolute defeat. It is dusk. I am feeling trapped by unwelcome certainties, even as the thought of failure and loss already is giving way to relief and acceptance. To this picture my generous, refurbishing memory, has now added my newly widowed mother waiting for me at the back door with a frank, consoling smile—a pat on the shoulder. And somehow memory has, completely unaccountably, allowed me still to be in my silver-and-blue uniform, my high unwieldy cleats, my silver helmet hanging at my knees.

Quitting, of course, when it actually came, was never so dramatic. I wasn't dropped or ruled off the field or jeered at for not being good enough. There was no big scene. Merely one day I was "out" for football and practicing, then the next day, or some other day, I wasn't, and life had begun then in the new direction it would go—the direction leading to here.

There is no shame in this. No blemish on football's permanent record, and not on mine. Other boys returned the next day, fought, drilled, tackled, caught passes, grew abstracted, suffered, were defeated, and stayed. And I am sure that all the ways I felt at my lowest, most unjoined were ways they felt, too. Except they somehow managed to find the heart of the game, became tuned-in to the coaching, allowed themselves to be provoked instead of bemused by the chance of failure versus success. This was a watershed event, no doubt, a definite dividing line in my life; but perhaps it was not a line between one kind of character and another, less good one, but only between what made them football players and me not.

To realize at a young age, and without heartbreak or profound loss that you simply are not always going to be in on "the big thing," that you are not good enough at something and therefore must get used to it (this time, anyway), and that there are important things you can and must get along without—all this makes a good lesson, one worth learning, inasmuch as it is resolutely true, and its truth breeds sympathy and compassion for oneself and becomes a road marker on the way to unexpected resourcefulness. This lesson seems to me one clear, shining value of sport, and it was football, so long ago now, that taught it to me.

SCOTT OSTLER

JOE MONTANA, KING OF COOL

The greatest quarterback in the history of the Super Bowl always seemed oblivious to the pressure

FROM SUPER BOWL XXX

I T IS THE FRIDAY NIGHT BEFORE Super Bowl XVI and eastern Michigan is frozen stiff.

The San Francisco 49ers hit Pontiac early in the week and Pontiac hit back, with blizzards and wind-chill temperatures of 50-below.

Joe Montana, who threw a miracle touchdown pass to beat the Cowboys and put the 49ers into their first Super Bowl, is behind the wheel of an NFL courtesy car. Dwight Clark, who caught that pass with the tips of his finger, is riding shotgun.

After dinner, the boys are returning to the team's hotel, but Montana takes a detour. He drives into a mall parking lot. It is dark and empty, a vast sheet of icy blacktop.

Montana punches the accelerator, gives a series of sharp cranks to the steering wheel, and sends the car skidding and spinning in full circles, sliding past light poles, careening into banks of soft snow, a carnival thrill ride that has jumped its tracks.

Coach Bill Walsh has made it clear he wants his players to be loose and have fun while gearing up for the big game, but Clark is pretty sure this isn't what Walsh has in mind.

A Southern lad new to the snow, Clark is scared silly. He braces his hands against the dashboard and stares at Montana, who glances at Clark, laughs with glee, and gives the wheel another spin.

So much for the theory that Joe Montana became the greatest Super Bowl performer of all time by locking himself into a Zen-like trance before games.

There are many other theories: Joe was motivated by fear and insecurity.

Joe was supremely confident.

Joe cared more than anyone else.

Joe cared less than anyone else.

Joe was a space alien who stepped out of a UFO.

This much is clear: Montana had a serious gap in his sports education. He never learned how to choke, and by the time he arrived at his first Super Bowl it was too late to learn.

Joe and the 49ers would win that game, and three more Super Bowls, and Montana would be the game's MVP three times.

Montana's four-game career would stamp him as the NFL's ultimate Super Bowl performer, and maybe the ultimate championship-game guy in any sport.

"He allowed everyone on his team to capture what we all want, to conquer the ultimate moment," says Ronnie Lott, a defensive back on all four of those Super Bowl teams. "But Joe was the only guy to do it routinely."

In four games, a legend was made.

Super Bowl XVI
January 24, 1982—Pontiac, Michigan
49ers 26, Bengals 21

The most vivid memory I have of Joe Montana the week before

his first Super Bowl game is that I have no vivid memory of Joe Montana.

This bland and low-key young man was football's new Mr. Excitement? We media angle-mongers, looking for the young star with the cool name, were disappointed.

As a subspecies of player, quarterbacks tend to have large personalities, to hold court, to be gold mines of quotes, quips, and controversy. Joe Namath, Joe Theismann, Terry Bradshaw, Jim McMahon, guys such as that would play the media like a very large violin. Not Montana.

He later admitted he was wary of the press, afraid he might be misquoted or accidentally say something that might fire up the opposition. So he talked and talked that week, and said nothing.

Instead of dominating the Super Bowl hype, Montana eased into the game as quietly as a fan sneaking into the stadium.

Joe never did talk a good game, and maybe that helps explain why 81 players were drafted ahead of him in 1979. This guy is going to step into an NFL huddle and lead 10 other men into battle?

The Happy Dummies, that's what offensive lineman Randy Cross named this 49ers team, because most of the players were too young and naive to be intimidated by the Super Bowl. To them, this was a bonus game. They were in Pontiac to have fun, and they worked hard at it.

Walsh gave his players a curfew but never bothered to enforce it, assuming incorrectly that the severe weather would limit their adventures. Some of the veterans were alarmed at the kids' loosey-goosey attitude and late hours. Offensive tackle Keith Fahnhorst stood up during a Friday team meeting and suggested that the players self-impose an 11 p.m. curfew for the final two nights.

Rookie cornerback Lott cleared his throat and said, "Look, I think we should just keep doing what we've been doing, because it's working."

And did it really matter? NFL experts agreed that the Bengals had the superior team—bigger, tougher, more talented, more experienced. No amount of sleep by the 49ers was going to bridge those gaps.

The 49ers' only hope was some kind of strange magic, and that's where Joe Montana came in. You couldn't quite write off this team because you couldn't quite get a handle on its quarterback.

Montana was a third-round draft pick two seasons earlier and, though he started seven games in 1980 and all 16 in '81, he still was regarded as an inconsistent quarterback with a mediocre arm.

But he had a certain poise and ability to make plays, and people were starting to notice. During Super Bowl week Montana was featured on the covers of *Time* ("Super Dreams"), *Newsweek* (with Bengals quarterback Ken Anderson, "Duel of Wits"), and *Sports Illustrated* ("Gunning for Glory").

Joe's teammates still were learning about the quiet kid from Notre Dame. They knew he did not rattle easily. He brought the 49ers back from a 28-point deficit to beat New Orleans in 1980, and there was the NFC Championship Game against Dallas in San Francisco. Was it just luck, or was a trend developing?

The 49ers knew Montana was hungry to play. In a midseason game in which he was struggling, Walsh ordered backup quarterback Guy Benjamin to take over for the next offensive series.

The 49ers' defense intercepted a pass, but Benjamin couldn't find his helmet. While he searched frantically, Montana dashed onto the field, huddled the team, and threw a touchdown pass.

"That's classic Montana," Benjamin says, laughing. "That's how he responded."

The 49ers knew their quarterback's quiet off-field personality would change in the heat of battle. Before the NFC title game, Dallas defensive end Ed (Too Tall) Jones told the media that the Cowboys did not respect the 49ers. That Sunday, Montana pump-faked Jones into the air, zinged a touchdown pass, and jumped into Jones' face screaming, "Respect that, [expletive deleted]!"

But now Montana was in the Super Bowl, and all previous bets were off. Was the famed touchdown pass to Clark a fluke? Was Montana for real? Could he handle the pressure of sudden fame? Could he respond in the biggest game?

As game day approached, the 49ers tried to get a read on the kid. The only overt sign of leadership was when he suggested that

Walsh play a recording of the Kenny Loggins song "This Is It" in the locker room before the game, for inspiration.

Other than that...

"None of us knew for sure how Joe would react in the big game," Keith Fahnhorst says. "Some promising young quarterbacks have been destroyed by bad Super Bowl games. Watching Joe that week, you couldn't tell, you weren't sure what you were seeing."

Lott tried to read Montana's eyes, looking for fear or confidence. He would watch Montana and wonder, "Is he ready?"

On game day, some of the 49ers went to the Silverdome early in taxis, but most took the team bus, which got stuck in a traffic jam caused by the motorcade of Vice President George Bush and Secretary of Transportation (ah, the irony) Andrew Lewis.

On the bus, to break the tension, Walsh pretended to listen to the Super Bowl play-by-play on radio, giving his players mock updates from the Silverdome. Great news: The 49ers, quarterbacked by their equipment manager, have just taken the lead.

When the bus reached the stadium 20 minutes before pregame warmups, the 49ers didn't have time to think about being nervous. The team was thrilled just to be reunited.

The 49ers opened their Super Bowl era with two long touchdown drives that were perfect examples of the Walsh-Montana chemistry. The 49ers' offense was a mystical jigsaw puzzle of formations and complex quarterback reads, more confusing to learn and operate than any other scheme in football. And just a few days before the game, Walsh had added several new wrinkles.

He had discovered that it was almost impossible to overload the football brain of Montana. Walsh knew that if he showed Montana a blueprint of the Eiffel Tower before a game, Joe and his guys would have it built by halftime.

On their first possession, the 49ers marched to a touchdown. The big play was a 14-yard pass off a fake reverse that was installed in the playbook only days before. The 49ers made it 14-0 in the second quarter when Montana threw an 11-yard touchdown pass to running back Earl Cooper, using an unbalanced line that the Bengals had not seen because the 49ers had not used it.

146

In the second half, the Bengals battled back and began over-powering the 49ers. What saved San Francisco, Walsh is convinced, was Montana's poise and absolute refusal to crack. When the 49ers' lead shrank to 6 points early in the fourth quarter, Montana led a field-goal drive that iced the game.

Lott, Fahnhorst, and the other 49ers now knew what kind of quarterback they had on their hands.

The media descended upon Joe Montana, the game's MVP, and he didn't have a lot to say.

Super Bowl XIX
January 20, 1985—Stanford, California
49ers 38, Dolphins 16

Many players have risen to an occasion, but few have levitated above it.

A few years after Super Bowl XIX, Montana told me that when he walked onto the Stanford Stadium field, he had felt a strange lightness, as if he were floating above the grass on a cloud.

The roar of the hometown crowd lifted him even higher.

"The only other time I felt the energy of a crowd that strong," he said, "was when I went on stage with Huey Lewis and the News."

That happened when Montana was coaxed out of a concert audience to sing back-up on the song "It's Hip To Be Square," which could have been Joe's theme song. Even though he drove a Ferrari, was married to a beautiful actress/model, and enjoyed heroic status in San Francisco, he was still just one of the guys.

In this game, Montana wasn't even supposed to be the hippest quarterback on the field, and that gave him something he had in each of his four Super Bowls—an almost desperate need to prove something.

The three main focuses of media attention the week of Super Bowl XIX were, in no particular order: Dan Marino, Dan Marino, and Dan Marino.

Or so it seemed to the 49ers and to Montana, who quietly seethed.

The Dolphins' amazing second-year quarterback passed for

5,084 yards and 48 touchdowns during the 1984 regular season, both NFL records. Montana logged a mere 3,630 yards and 28 touchdowns.

All the buzz was over young Marino.

"Maybe you're selling our defense short," was all Montana said to the press in response to Marinomania.

The other 49ers loved it. They knew Joe would be inspired because he was almost maniacally competitive.

Safety Tom Holmoe tells of going to a team party at Montana's home and watching Joe play a teammate in a friendly tennis match that became a life-and-death struggle.

Now Montana felt the unspoken challenge of his rival quarterback. He was simmering, wondering why nobody seemed to notice that he and Walsh had the 49ers' offense polished and clicking with a precision that made a Rolex watch look like a high school metal-shop project.

No way Montana could match Marino's cannon-for-an-arm strength, but passing is a lot like real estate—location is everything. Montana once told Dwight Clark that when Clark had his back turned to a defensive back, he (Joe) would throw the ball a few inches to the right or left of Clark's midsection, to indicate the direction Clark should spin to elude the defender.

Clark laughed, assuming Montana was kidding. Nobody could throw a football that accurately. Montana wasn't kidding.

The 49ers not only had Montana, they had the strongest team they would field in the decade, so they entered the game with what Randy Cross calls "justifiable arrogance."

Marino was impressive, leading the Dolphins to advantages of 3-0 and 10-7. But his cleats were in the turf, while Montana floated above, passing for a Super Bowl-record 331 yards. He completed 24 of 35 passing attempts for 3 touchdowns and ran the ball 5 times for 59 yards.

On one play, Clark was Montana's fourth option as a receiving target. Clark drew tight coverage running downfield, so he wasn't even looking for the pass that nearly hit him in the head. Somehow he caught the ball.

"When I came back to the huddle," Clark says, "Joe was laughing. He knew he'd surprised me."

Surprised a lot of people. Montana was the game's most valuable player.

Super Bowl XXIII
January 22, 1989—Miami, Florida
49ers 20, Bengals 16

Sportswriters love a good soap opera, and now we had one before Super Bowl XXIII.

There was tension and turmoil on the 49ers. Walsh had hinted that Montana, at 32, was nearing the end of his career and soon would need to be phased out, especially considering the emergence of backup Steve Young as a potential star.

Walsh later confided that if Young had been able to beat the Cardinals while subbing for the injured Montana in November, he would have replaced Montana as the starting quarterback. The 49ers lost the game by 1 point.

Joe saw the vultures circling, waiting for his football carcass. This would have been a dramatic game for him to make a statement regarding the true nature of greatness, but the 49ers were so much better than the Bengals that it seemed doubtful any Montana heroics would be necessary.

Or that was the considered opinion of the experts of the media, who are trained to know these things.

Supreme confidence served the 49ers in two previous Super Bowls, but this time it backfired. As time ticked away, the 49ers found themselves in a Mission Impossible situation:

With 3:10 left, they trailed the Bengals 16-13, taking possession on their 8-yard line. That scraping sound you heard was the Bengals' "SWAT Team" defense digging in.

On the 49ers' sideline, Ronnie Lott told himself, "No way Joe can do it," but that was Lott's mental game. He would utter that phrase and challenge Montana to prove him wrong.

The 49ers huddled in their own end zone to wait out a long TV time out. Tackle Harris Barton was verging on meltdown.

"I'm nervous and tight, and I'm goin' off," Barton recalls. "I'm telling everyone, 'We gotta win!' Joe says, 'Hey, H., look down there above the far corner of the end zone. There's John Candy!'

"I look and sure enough, there's John Candy, eating popcorn." The tension seemed to leak out of the huddle as 11 players turned to watch the fat comedian enjoying a snack. Then the 49ers began to work their way downfield like a marching band.

With 1:22 left and the ball on the Bengals' 35, the pressure got to Montana. His breathing became labored as he tried to shout plays above the roar of the crowd. He feared he would hyperventilate.

He threw the ball away, his only incompletion on the 92-yard drive. After a 10-yard penalty, he passed 27 yards to Jerry Rice, 8 yards to Roger Craig, and, to win it, a 10-yard dart to John Taylor for a touchdown with 34 seconds remaining.

If you had to pull three minutes out of Montana's career to present as credentials for admission to Valhalla, these would be the three.

Joe's totals for the day: 23 completions in 36 attempts for 357 yards and 2 touchdown passes, both in the fourth quarter.

In the losers' locker room, wide receiver Cris Collinsworth offered a simple explanation:

"Montana is not human."

Super Bowl XXIV
January 28, 1990—New Orleans
49ers 55, Broncos 10

It's fascinating to watch the evolution of a player and a team over a decade.

Montana had gone from a beach-apartment guy to a land baron who had a reproduction of the Sistine Chapel's ceiling mural painted in his living room.

He had gone from a carefree, approachable dude to a businessman walled in by responsibilities of wealth and fame. Want to see Joe? Make an appointment.

He carried around enough superstar baggage to require a forklift. The week before the game, one of Montana's two ex-wives said nasty things about him in a supermarket tabloid. A television reporter fed Montana to the rumor mill with unsubstantiated allegations that the league was covering up knowledge of drug abuse by three NFL quarterbacks, not named.

Montana's response: "Why should I worry about a bunch of crap?"

San Francisco fans, who had been so giddy over a first Super Bowl victory, now were spoiled by success, and had helped drive Walsh into retirement.

Only a few battered warriors remained from the original Happy Dummies.

Montana had played his greatest regular season ever and was voted the league's MVP, but he knew age was chasing him, and he was determined to prove he still was Joe Montana.

By now, we geniuses of the media finally had it nailed down: Joe was under siege; the opponent was in deep trouble.

In the Superdome, TV cameras were set up in each locker room to record the postgame scene, and when the 49ers arrived for the game, Montana put on a headset and pretended to be a camera operator.

"I've never seen anyone so on as he was against Denver," says Dwight Clark. "The right reads, the accuracy of the passes, just phenomenal."

It was his final great Super Bowl concert: 22 completions in 29 passing attempts, 297 yards, 5 touchdowns, a third most-valuable-player award.

Four games, four unique challenges, four 49ers triumphs, and four near-perfect performances by Joe Montana.

His Super Bowl statistics: 122 pass attempts, 83 completions, 1,142 yards, 11 touchdowns, and, against the most dogged and desperate defenses the AFC could throw at him, zero interceptions.

Terry Bradshaw led the Steelers to four Super Bowl victories in four tries, but he didn't have Montana's numbers. Roger Staubach threw 8 touchdown passes in his four Super Bowls but was intercepted 4 times and the Cowboys were 2-2.

"Clearly Joe was the best quarterback who ever played, no question," Walsh says. "Terry was a magnificent quarterback, but I don't think he could have done what Joe did—take that first band of young guys, with so little firepower, and win it all."

Along with the obvious physical skills, what Montana brought to the big game was an almost unearthly cool, something almost hypnotic and certainly contagious. To a man, the 49ers say they handled the pressure better because of the confidence radiating from their quarterback.

"The more pressure, the calmer he was," Fahnhorst says, "and it would rub off on everyone. To see him perform so well under pressure helped us cope, and made us all expect more out of ourselves."

Montana's father, Joe Sr., says his son learned to be cool under fire when he was in grammar school and played on a highly competitive all-star traveling basketball team, coached by Joe Sr.

But Joe's dad searches his memory and can't come up with even one instance of his son folding under pressure, not even back in the very beginning of his athletic career.

So it seems that young Joe didn't so much learn to deal with pressure, but that he was born with the knack.

"It's simple," Montana's pal Huey Lewis says. "It can be overanalyzed, but it's like an eleven-year-old kid playing ball in the street, loving each play, and each play is its own game. He's not thinking of results. He doesn't care about the score or an interception. He just throws because now the next play is all that matters."

Harris Barton more or less supports that theory. "Joe went out to have a good time. Every game was like a high school game to him." Ronnie Lott adds, "Sometimes a guy's just a normal guy, but he's got a Microsoft brain."

Maybe the reason Montana was the anti-sound bite, the man without a colorful quote, was that he was trying to tell us something. It might have sounded like this:

"There's nothing profound to say. It's just a football game."

SCOTT MOMADAY

ATHLETE IN A STATE OF GRACE

There are few moments more memorable
than when form and function come together
in unison on a playing field

FROM SUPER BOWL XXX

Pentathlon athletes are the most beautiful men
in Greece—they are as strong as they are swift.
                                        —*Aristotle*

I always have admired the phrase "state of grace." It is, for me,
a concept that holds high promise and infinite possibility. In
a state of grace, one stands on the verge of extraordinary
achievement, the realization of something nearly beyond mortali-
ty. In my parochial childhood, the phrase implied a religious cir-
cumstance, a condition of innocence or spiritual zeal. But it is,
rather, as in the words of Aristotle, an equation of aesthetic distinction and physical prowess—beauty and action, if you will,
form and function in exceptional union and unique expression. In
a sense this is a valid definition of sport, of athletic competition.

ATHLETE IN A STATE OF GRACE

To witness the performance of an athlete in a state of grace is to remember it forever. Here are a few I remember.

On a summer evening in Arizona, I climbed into the stands above the track. It was dusk. In a few minutes the track and the infield were flooded with bright light. People were coming into the stands, but the crowd was sparse. The runners had begun to appear from the dressing rooms. There was a general excitement, a vague, delicious tension on the evening air. I felt that something remarkable was about to happen. And so it was.

When Edwin Moses appeared, walking into the pools of light, there was a murmur that grew into cheers and applause, not wild, but almost restrained. Moses was nearing the end of his long, remarkable string of victories in the 400-meter hurdles. In the course of his walk, which was stately, he kicked high, then he pumped his knees, and broke into a jog. But these seemed all one motion, the definition of a stride, a natural procession of parts that were precisely equal to the sum, indeed which were the sum. And I could not tell where in the sequence the walk became a sprint. The race was a movement in the symphony, an integrated stanza, not more exceptional than the walk-on or the victory lap.

Another moment that I can recall at will: I was an undergraduate at the University of New Mexico. Our team was called the Lobos, and our colors were cherry and silver. Was it a homecoming game? I don't remember. I don't remember the opposing team. What I remember is that at one point in the course of the game there was a decisive moment. We had Don Perkins in the backfield. His jersey, number 43, later was retired, and he went on to a distinguished career with the Dallas Cowboys.

The play I remember began when Perkins broke wide and streaked down the sideline as the quarterback glided deep in the pocket. The quarterback's protection was momentary, and he waited as long as he could to release the ball. I think it might have been the longest pass I ever saw thrown in a college game. I thought with a sinking heart that it was overthrown.

But there was something in the look of the receiver that placed all of probability in suspension. When Perkins drew even with my seat on the 40-yard line, the ball appeared to be at its zenith, and directly over him. I was in the silence that precedes frenzy.

Perkins ran by me, the frozen strain of purpose on his face, his eyes nearly closed. I could hear his footsteps; the stutter bore no real relation to his speed. I could hear his breathing, labored exhalations only, like the echo of his cleats on the grass. He blurred, and then I watched his back hurtling towards the goal line. Literally in the nick of time, he turned his head and shoulders slightly, extended his body, reached, and took the ball on his fingertips. And somewhere in this series of extremes he crossed the goal line and the edge of time. Or so it seemed to me; he stood alone, exultant in the general disbelief, in a dimension of timelessness.

These moments have existed in the Super Bowl, too. Super Bowl X was one of these, and it stands out in my mind. It was the Orange Bowl; it was the bicentennial year (1976); and it was a classic matchup. The Dallas Cowboys were the first wild-card team to reach the Super Bowl. They had gone 10-4 in the regular season, finishing a game behind St. Louis in the NFC East. They upset Minnesota 17-14 in the NFC divisional playoffs on a last-minute pass (the fabled "Hail Mary") from quarterback Roger Staubach to Drew Pearson. Then, in the NFC Championship Game, they trounced the Los Angeles Rams 37-7. The Cowboys were a team of speed and finesse; they did not beat up their opponents; rather they deceived and bedazzled them. The Pittsburgh Steelers, on the other hand, played old-fashioned, bruising football. The Steelers had gone 12-2 in the regular season, and they had dispatched Baltimore and Oakland in the playoffs. With Franco Harris running the ball and Joe Greene anchoring the defense, Pittsburgh had put together 11 consecutive victories before losing its final regular-season game on the way to Miami. The crisp air of that January afternoon bore a scent of bitter rivalry. The two teams had come to do battle; there was no love lost between them.

The Cowboys struck first. From the Steelers' 29, following the recovery of a bobbled punt snap, Staubach lofted the ball to Pearson. Pearson took the ball in stride and raced into the end zone. But it did not seem a race. It seemed a long moment in which all speed and exertion were smoothed out in slow motion. There seemed no hurry, nothing extraneous to the perfect errand of crossing the goal line. It was choreography; it was a work of art. It was a performance that justified Super Bowl X.

But the best was still to come. Dallas led 7-0 in the first quarter, 10-7 at halftime, and 10-9 in the fourth quarter. Then the lead changed hands. It was 12-10, then 15-10, Pittsburgh. The momentum swung, until there were less than 5 minutes play.

The Steelers' number 88, an acrobatic young receiver named Lynn Swann, made the decisive play of the game. He ran downfield, abandoned his route, and glided into the deep middle. Pittsburgh quarterback Terry Bradshaw threw long, and as the ball was in the air, he was hit and knocked unconscious. He did not see Swann's catch, but everyone else did. Swann cradled the ball in his arms at the Cowboys' 5. Cornerback Mark Washington hit him from behind, but Swann barely stumbled, regained his stride, and scored. It was the touchdown that won the game 21-17. The reception was pure choreography, a work of art.

On that afternoon I was privileged to see the finest coordination of mind and muscle, of speed and balance, of power and grace. But what comes back to me in memory is another incredible catch by Swann. Deep in his territory, Bradshaw faded and threw long. Swann sped along the right sideline. In an instant of pure suspension he leaped for the ball, taking it in his fingers. He seemed impossibly high above the field. Washington also jumped for the ball. The ball deflected off both men's hands and spun into the air. Swann came down on his right shoulder, sliding forward and at the same time rolling over on his back. The ball plummeted, and he took it easily, gently in his grasp. It was a whole and singular act, its own justification, committed in a state of grace.

It may be that today, here on this field, a man in the balance of strength and swiftness, an athlete in a state of grace, will perform such feats as these.

Let us hope so.

Let us expect it.

JOHN WIEBUSCH

GOOSE BUMPS

To one who worked alongside him,
NFL Commissioner Pete Rozelle reflected all
that is right with the world of football

FROM SUPER BOWL XXXI

H E NEVER LIKED THE WORD "SUPER." He thought it was corny, a cliché. But the name stuck to the game he found-ed because it fit.

He never liked the word "super." But it fit something else, too. For 29 years, and more, he was our Superman.

Pete Rozelle's phone booth was an office on Park Avenue in New York. His super powers included his remarkable persuasiveness. He had the rare gift of making the subject of his conversations feel as if he or she were the only person who mattered. Incredibly, he even managed to do this when he spoke to groups.

I joined NFL Properties in December, 1970, and I witnessed my first Pete Rozelle press conference on the Friday before Super Bowl V in Miami. I stood in the back of the room at the Fontainebleau Hotel, and what I saw left me breathless. He not only answered the questions, but he expanded on them. He got laughs when he wanted them, and he got applause when the session ended.

I never missed another Super Bowl Friday press address, and he rode the waves with consummate style.

Me, I always stood in the back of the room, as if being there would hide my goose bumps.

You don't stay with the same employer for decades unless there is a good reason. Pete Rozelle was the initial good reason for Pete Abitante, Greg Aiello, Joe Browne, Joel Bussert, Roger Goodell, Bill Granholm, Peter Hadhazy, Jim Heffernan, Dick Maxwell, Val Pinchbeck, Jim Steeg, and Don Weiss, among others.

Pete had an old Underwood typewriter in his office, and he used it to write friendly notes to all of us. A more sensitive big boss never existed. I have a folder of his notes. I think we all do.

In 1990, I interviewed Pete for the background that became a foreword to a twenty-fifth anniversary Super Bowl book we were doing for Simon & Schuster.

We were finishing the session in his office, which overlooked the sylvan stables of Gene Klein and Wayne Lucas in Rancho Santa Fe, California, and he was pouring me yet another cup of coffee.

"You know, you have a great job," he said. "If someone had asked me forty years ago which job in the NFL I'd like to have, I'd have said yours."

"Yeah," I said, "and if someone had asked me which job I wanted, I would have said yours!"

He laughed loudly. "I really mean it," he said. "Print was the most exciting thing to me then, and I still love reading all the media I can get my hands on."

I asked him about the house he and his wife Carrie were building in the hills of Rancho Santa Fe. I asked if we could drive by it, and he gave me directions from the passenger's seat. "The house is just so big," he said. "It's so big it's embarrassing."

"You deserve a big house," I said. I glanced at him and he was shaking his head.

The framed house was not so much large as sprawling. Mostly, it had understated style. Like him. His embarrassment was a cover for his modesty.

He thanked me for coming down from Los Angeles. He told me he appreciated my taking time out of my busy schedule. He said he looked forward to seeing the book, although he knew he would like it. And I know he meant every word he said.

Eighteen months earlier, in his final days as commissioner after his surprise retirement at the March owners' meetings, I had a valedictory interview with him in his office in New York.

Understated style...the office was the epitome of it. Lamps and leather couches and chairs, a simple but elegant desk table. And, in a flashback to an earlier time, that old Underwood behind the desk. His personal notes always were typed in hunt-and-peck lower case and almost always closed with: "cheers," and a simple "Pete" signature. The office looked exactly as it did the first time I saw it 19 years before.

"This is a great office," I said. "But it never really has shown off the trappings of your success."

"I like simple solutions to this kind of thing," he said, waving his arm around a part of the room. "Trophies and awards and that kind of stuff just aren't me."

Later that morning, I asked how someone as sensitive as he was had been able to control the egos of NFL owners, beginning with the patriarchs such as Halas, Marshall, and Rooney, and continuing on through the young Turks who had come into the league in the 1980s after paying a lot of money for their franchises.

"I treated them all with respect," he said. "I never forgot who they were. But I also never forgot that I worked for the league in general and not for a club in particular."

He championed revenue sharing from the beginning, and the league prospered in small markets as well as large ones, with television monies and profits from NFL Properties and NFL Films divided equally.

It worked.

And everyone prospered.

GOOSE BUMPS

The last time I saw him was at an awards dinner in New York six or seven years later, six or eight months after he had undergone brain surgery. He had lost most of his hair and he looked tired. But that light-up-the-room smile still was there, and he rose from his chair to greet me. We talked about the Cowboys and the 49ers and about Carrie and Rancho Santa Fe, and he asked me how things were in Los Angeles. Then we said goodby.

I meant to drop him a note in his final months, before he died in December 1999, but I never did. I know he'll see this:

```
dear pete,
      i think you know how i feel about what it
was like to work for you and with you for two
decades and to have known you for close to three.
      but i wanted to tell you, anyway.
i wanted you to know that you always made me so
proud. the worlds of sports and entertainment
are a richer place, literally and figuratively,
because
you were there.
      you were...well, super.
cheers,
```

ANDREI CODRESCU

ON FOOTBALL...
AND INNOCENCE

A transplant to America found many
attributes of his adopted home embodied in
the games played on Sunday afternoon

FROM SUPER BOWL XXXI

I T WAS THE FINAL MINUTE of my first football game. The score
was tied and the Saints were trying a 50-yard field-goal attempt. When Morten Andersen stepped in, the crowd became
full of something I can only describe as religious fervor. Andersen's foot was being charged by the mystical wish of the crowd,
like some sort of icon. I was reminded of the way villagers in parts
of Mexico look up to religious statues, pinning all their wishes for
good health and success to the worn plaster. Only this was no ancient statue; this was the living foot of a fairly young person, and
we were looking down at it. And then it happened: Morten made
the kick and the Saints won. The crowd went wild, and I learned,
as I would in repeated performances over the years, that Morten
Andersen's foot was the icon. What's more, it was well worth wor-
shipping because little else about that particular Saints team was.

ON FOOTBALL...AND INNOCENCE

It was my son, Lucian, who introduced me to the religion of football. Before moving to New Orleans, we lived in Baltimore during the dark ages—after the Colts left and before the Ravens arrived. Talk of football rang hollow in that city back then. A few weeks after the Colts' departure, I saw a throng of men outside Johnny Unitas's Golden Arm restaurant, looking as if they were in mourning.

Sports fans in Baltimore threw themselves passionately into baseball, the city's other major pastime. My son, who played Little League baseball, made it a point to discuss with me all the finer points of the game and the various personality traits of each Orioles player. He explained this to me very slowly, the way you would explain nuclear physics to an ape. The reason for his concern was simple: I was handicapped. I was born in Romania, a country without baseball, football, Little League, or trading cards. I had had the unspeakably bad fortune of spending an entire childhood without any of these things.

Don't get me wrong. We had sports. There was soccer, above all. Soccer was a national pastime of major proportions. At the time, Romania was a communist country. There was little besides sports that anyone could discuss openly and publicly. You couldn't argue about politics or history or even geography. All those areas were subject to the communist party line. Only soccer escaped the careful monitoring of the commissars. Our newspapers were full of lies on every page except the last—the sports page.

There was something else, too: I was a reader. In the kind of world I grew up in, guys with glasses and guys with muscles didn't mix. I remember coming home, with books under my arm, one evening after the soccer game. An angry crowd was heading my way. The people were angry because the home team had lost. Much beer had been drunk. But they didn't sound appeased. They needed a substantial sacrifice, something with glasses. I managed to get behind one of the huge medieval doors on a side street, and cowered there until they passed.

I have thought about this often, and every time I have thought about it, I thanked my lucky stars that my children grew up in

America. Both my boys have an appetite for sports. They played baseball and football, and they took karate. And both of them also like to read. Their sports activities did not reflect one way or another on their intellectual pursuits. Or vice-versa. There is little or no prejudice in this country against developing both body and mind.

I saw my first baseball game in Baltimore, and my first football game in New Orleans. Five years stretched between these two events. I consider my first baseball game my true induction to American citizenship. In fact, I received citizenship just around the time I saw that game. My son explained the game to me and taught me how to watch it. I kept following the ball at all times and had no idea why there was so much time between one pitch and the next. I had no idea why all those people were just standing around on the field. There was so much time between batted balls, I spent a lot of time daydreaming. I could have a read a book, too, if it had not been for my vestigial fear of crowds. It was a perfect blue-sky summer day. Baseball was dreamy and good-natured and I took that as a perfect symbol for American tolerance.

Five years later, I took it pretty much for granted that I was becoming more American all the time. America was tolerant, it was true, but it was also aggressive, goal-oriented, fiercely competitive, and ritualistic. Some of these qualities impinged on tolerance. As I looked around me, I saw also that the America of the nineties was not as good-natured as America of the seventies. In the seventies, you could daydream and read books and hope that inflation wouldn't totally eat your earnings. In the nineties, a whole host of worries had descended upon us. There was a new world economy with lots of insecurity. Immigrants were suddenly looked upon as enemies of hard-working Americans, instead of hard-working Americans-to-be. America, a country of hard-working immigrants, was becoming a country of walls and borders, of fear and suspicion.

Football had lots to teach me about surviving in the tougher new world around me. From the first, it was clear that daydreaming was out. The action was fast, rough, and relentless. Each yard was fought for with brutish strength. The strategic considerations were complex and had been thought about in advance, though they took only seconds to execute.

I found all that quite apt, both for the times and for myself. This was the era of corporate buyouts, when big fish ate little fish, when unabashed partisans of raw capitalism fought to conquer more and more territory. Many of these new breed of aggressive entrepreneurs took for their symbols predators such as "eagles." Some of them were corporate "raiders." I was quite taken by this analogy, but when I told it to my oldest son, he laughed at me. "How about the Dolphins?" he said. "How about the Cardinals? There is nothing aggressive about them."

In the mid-eighties, the Saints were coming out of a series of bad years, and there was an atmosphere of cautious hope in New Orleans. I don't know about other cities, but in New Orleans, the Saints are regarded with all the superstitious passion befitting their name. The team song is "When the Saints Come Marching In." People have been known to pray to such local saints as St. Expedite for their favorite team. This St. Expedite is supposed to hurry things up when they are too slow to believe. Well, patience wore thin quite a few times with the home team.

In New Orleans, the city of Mardi Gras, where people express themselves through masks and costumes, feelings didn't take long to dress up. At games, people clad in the most egregious colors prayed loudly for touchdowns. There were tortured clowns, suffering martyrs, even penitents with whips and crosses. At one point years earlier, the long-suffering folk took to wearing paper bags over their heads with the motto WHO DAT? This is the local way of saying, "Who is that? Who are you?" One might recognize in such a cry the exasperation of a parent when a child just can't seem to bring home that passing grade.

It was my luck to be there for a Saints victory. My son, who had studied the chances for this game with the dedication of a scientist, was convinced that victory was ours. People around us were less certain. A large woman in gold and black, waxed philosophical between bites of a Lucky Dog with everything on it. "God will-in', this might be the day!" she said. So when Morten Andersen's miraculous foot made everyone's hopes come true, there was more than satisfaction. There was jubilation.

I was hooked, to my distress. Every Sunday for the next year I turned into Homo Americanus, or the Couch Potato with the long-neck in one hand. My sons were, at first, my patient pals and teachers, even when I showed a complete lack of education concerning things such as "safeties" or "touchbacks."

To tell the truth, I felt quite inadequate. At one point, my youngest son, quite exasperated by the failing performances of the Saints, decided that I was the reason for their misfortune. "Dad," he said, "you've got to leave. Every time you're watching, there is an interception!" I was furious and about to bring down the full force of my patriarchal authority, but then I thought about it. Every time I left the room to get another beer, the team came back. As soon as I re-entered and started watching again, something horrible happened to them. Maybe my son was right.

My son is quite grown now, and I hope that he doesn't still think that I ruined it for the near-miss Saints of the early nineties. But maybe I did.

The trouble with getting older is that you begin to see the pattern. You know instinctively, when the season starts a certain way, how it's going to turn out. Still, you try to ignore that instinct because you're hoping for that surprise and pleasure you remember from your first game, when you were innocent.

I have been to quite a few football games since that first one, but with my sons gone on to their own lives, I don't get as much pleasure now. Still, the day the Saints win the Super Bowl, I'll rejoice without a thought. That day, my innocence will return.

JERRY KRAMER

MANY CHANGES, FEW DIFFERENCES

Thirty years later, a Packers star finds that the players are bigger and the salaries are better, but the road to victory is the same

FROM SUPER BOWL XXXI

I T HAS BEEN ALMOST 30 YEARS since I last strapped on a football helmet, since I last stuck my face into a defensive tackle's chest, since I last helped lead the Green Bay sweep, the trademark of Vince Lombardi's Packers. I don't weigh any more than I did then, but the weight has been redistributed.

My playing days are behind me, but football still is a part of our household. As I write this, and the NFL season moves toward the playoffs that lead to Super Bowl XXXI, it is the last week of football for most high schools and many colleges. My youngest son, Jordan, is playing high school football; his brother, Matt, is playing college football.

Their older sister, Alicia, reminds me of the Thanksgiving dinner 10 or 11 years ago when I was sitting at the head of the table and asked everyone to give thanks. I said I was thankful for my family, for their health, and for the love that we shared. My wife Wink said she was thankful for grandma and grandpa. Alicia and Matt gave thanks for the good things in their lives. Finally we turned to Jordan, who was, I believe, 6 years old. After a long pause, Jordan said, in a very serious voice, "I'm thankful for the NFL."

Everyone laughed, but now, a decade later, I realize how much I share Jordan's feeling. I'm thankful for the NFL, too, thankful the league, Lombardi, and the Green Bay Packers allowed me to make a life with an extraordinary group of people, whom I also loved. The lessons I learned from Lombardi are forever in me and my children.

I also am thankful that football gives me a strong bond with my young sons.

Jordan competes on Friday for the Idaho State Championship. He plays for the Parma High School Panthers. Matt takes part on Saturday in the big intrastate collegiate game that matches his University of Idaho Vandals against the Boise State Broncos.

I grew up in Sandpoint, in northern Idaho. For the past 25 years, Wink and I have lived and raised our three children and several Chesapeake Bay retrievers on a 600-acre ranch along the Boise River, just outside of Parma. It's a long way from the excitement of New Orleans, New York, or even Green Bay. To much of the world, Boise, Idaho, is nowhere, and we live 40 miles from there, in a farming community of 1,700 people.

Wink and I drove to Pocatello to watch Parma face Glenns Ferry in the A-3 state championship game. The Panthers last won a conference title in 1978. Until 1996, Parma never had won a postseason playoff game.

Parma has only 19 players on its squad—11 starters, eight reserves. They've been together since grade school. The quarterback also plays on the defensive line. Almost everyone plays both ways. They're good kids—not loud, cocky or arrogant. They're solid young men with great work ethics.

This is football at its purest. It is about commitment, dedication, responsibility, discipline, consistency, love of the game—all the values Lombardi emphasized. No big bucks at this level. Nothing but hard work and sacrifice and dreams of glory. Come to think of it, it's not unlike Green Bay.

I see the kids pumping up each other, slapping each other, exhorting each other to play their best. In my mind, I see Ray Nitschke growling, and Fuzzy Thurston cheering, and Max McGee smiling, and I remember when we were all young and eager, full of optimism—full of fun, full of life, full of hope.

But that was then, and this is now, and I am as nervous as I was before Super Bowl I. Just like my playing days, I make three trips to the men's room before the kickoff.

Parma dominates Glenns Ferry, which had won 35 consecutive games. The final score is 26-6, a huge victory for the team and for the town. When the game ends, I find myself being congratulated for being a state champion, and I feel like one.

Early the next morning, Wink, Alicia, Jordan, and his friend and teammate, John Sexton, join me for the drive to Boise. This is the game of the year for both teams, Florida versus Florida State in miniature. I played for Idaho a million years ago. The Vandals' coach, Chris Tormey, asks me to say a few words to his players before the game.

The locker room is like a thousand other locker rooms I have entered—the clanking pads, the rolls of tape. It is a hot and humid room, crowded with very large bodies, bigger than my Green Bay teammates. The Vandals' offensive line averages between 280 and 285 pounds a man. We averaged 250 to 255. Forrest Gregg and I would have been little guys on this team.

I tell Matt and his teammates that football is a game of emotion, a game of attitude, of fire and ice: fire in your belly and ice on your mind. The mind must stay cool, analytical, calculating. No dumb penalties. No stupid mistakes. Harness that emotion.

I watch from the sidelines. Partly I want to be close to the action. Partly, I just don't want to use up a precious ticket. I need all I can get for my family and friends. Tickets for the game are scarce—unlike tickets for Super Bowl I. When we played Kansas City in the Coliseum in Los Angeles, there were about 30,000 empty seats.

The AFL-NFL World Championship Game wasn't quite Super yet.

The Vandals handle Boise State much better than we handled the Chiefs. Idaho builds a 55-6 lead, and coasts to a 64-19 victory.

What a weekend!

Sunday evening, the Packers are playing the Rams in St. Louis. I kick back in front of the big TV. The first half makes me feel lousy. The Rams lead 9-3. Green Bay seems to be playing tentatively, hesitantly. I shout advice at the TV set. Don't think. React. It's a game of abandon. Let your instincts take over. Caution to the wind. Let it happen. Make it happen.

My pep talk does the job again. The Packers rally in the second half and beat the Rams 24-9.

The weekend sets me thinking about football, about Green Bay, about the NFL. When I look at the NFL 30 years ago and the NFL today, a thought strikes me: Everything has changed, but nothing is different.

The players are bigger, stronger, faster, better athletes. One of my older sons, Dan, is a photojournalist. When he was searching the archives of the *Green Bay Press-Gazette*, he found a photo of me coming off the field. The caption refers to me as "Kramer, Gargantuan Guard." I also was known as "The Whale." I played at 255 pounds. That's a minnow today.

The players' bank accounts have grown, too. In my day, we didn't talk about our salaries. First, Lombardi forbid us to discuss our salaries. Second, we were embarrassed by how little we earned. Eight or nine years ago, I was playing golf at an NFL alumni outing in St. Louis, and I was with Ray Nitschke and John David Crow, an old teammate and an old opponent. I asked Ray, "What kind of bonus did you get as a rookie?"

I'd known Ray for more than a quarter of a century, but I still had no idea what he'd earned when we were teammates. He said, "I got five hundred, man." I said, "Damn, you doubled me. I only got two-fifty. I got $7,750 for the season and a $250 bonus." Ray opened his eyes wide and said, "You got eight thousand! I got only $7,700."

Another major difference in the game today is the media coverage. We used to have one writer from Green Bay and one from Milwaukee following us. We never had press conferences. The writers just wandered around the locker room talking to different guys. It wasn't like the swarm you see today. We had fun with the reporters. We weren't wary of them.

Of course, the coverage of the sport has grown tremendously, especially on television. With a satellite dish and a subscription to NFL Sunday Ticket, you can sit in front of a life-sized screen and flick back and forth among six or eight games and even watch more than one at a time.

And the Super Bowl has grown so much bigger than any of us possibly could have imagined. More people watch that game than saw us play in our entire careers.

But all these changes have taken place outside the lines. End zone to end zone, sideline to sideline, inside the playing field, nothing has changed. Not fundamentally, anyway.

You still need a great defense, a great offensive line, and a great running game to get to the Super Bowl. (I'm a little prejudiced about that offensive line part.) You still need the same qualities— commitment, preparation, discipline, courage, perseverance, a disdain for pain. You still learn the same lessons. Hard work does equate to success.

It's a huge step from high school football to college football, and another huge step to professional football. But it's still the same wonderful, demanding, rewarding, frustrating, exhilarating game.

I still love it.

Coach Lombardi once said, "All the rings, all the money, all the color, all the displays linger in the memory for only a short time and are soon gone, but the will to win, the will to excel, these are things that endure, and they are far more important than any of the events that occasion them."

Parma wins its first state championship. My alma mater wins the big game against Boise State. And the Packers beat the Rams.

What a weekend! And—icing on the cake—those damn Cowboys got beat!

AL MARTINEZ

OKAY, EVERBODY, COW DOWN!

*When the guys come over to watch the game on
Super Bowl Sunday, you don't serve caramel crisps
and watercress sandwiches*

FROM SUPER BOWL XXXII

E VERY YEAR, TO PROVE THAT I'm as macho as the dude next door, I watch the Super Bowl on television, unless I am fortunate enough to actually attend the game. I not only watch it, I invite some of the guys over to drink beer, dine on my cuisine (I mean chow down on my eats) and generally enjoy the 22 well-paid players on the screen attempting to flatten each other. For weeks prior to the day of the game I practice bellowing, barking, and shouting "WAY TO GO!" in order to blend in with the rest of the urban cowboys, mountain bikers, and dry wall plasterers. It's not easy.

In truth, I find it difficult being one of the guys, but I feel I somehow owe it to society to join 150 million other Americans in a tradition that has become as powerful as Christmas. It is a time of bonding not necessarily with one's family but with the men one would otherwise have nothing to do with the rest of the year. Think of it as a hitch in the military in which deep friendships are made and vows to meet years later are pledged and then forgotten the day you get your discharge papers.

I always have been a standoffish kind of guy, opting, for an evening with the L.A. Philharmonic or a jazz recital at the Hollywood Bowl over a poker game. I prefer a crisp coq de bruyere to burgers and fries and a nice bottle of vintage Blanquette de Limoux to a can of beer. And although it probably is the most popular food item on Super Bowl Sunday, I am emotionally incapable of eating pepperoni pizza, or any kind of pizza for that matter. It sticks in my throat when I try, and I'll be damned if I'll be strangled on my own dinner.

But I try to adjust. There are middle roads a guy can travel in the effort to abide by the Rules of Manhood, so each year on Super Bowl Sunday I open my Topanga house to every testosterone-oriented dude I know.

My wife, a gourmet cook, would rather watch Masterpiece Theater or the Wild World of Animals or Biography or an analysis of the trade war with Japan, anything but football. She leaves the house while The Game is in session. She similarly leaves to me the job of cooking, suggesting cheerfully that maybe us guys would just like raw knuckle bones to gnaw on instead of anything we actually might have to think about before eating.

I may be a little wry about Super Bowl Sunday but I do understand its importance in the American tradition. It plays a fundamental role in the conduct of our lives if only for this one day. Every Super Bowl Sunday, for instance, crime takes a dive, freeways and city streets are empty, and, I am told, fewer people die. I'm not all that sure that fewer people die. It may just be that no one is willing to haul the dead away until The Game is over.

I find it intriguing that crime is down during the game, suggesting that we all—drive-by shooters and church-going CPAs alike—are joined together in a mutuality of spirit for at least that one glorious day. It is a rewarding thought, unless one stops to think that the guy sitting next to you might be wanted in 12 states.

The first year I hosted a Super Bowl Sundayfest I didn't understand the rules. Topanga, which is a California community in the Santa Monica Mountains overlooking the Pacific Ocean, is a unique mix of artists, conservationists, and cowboys, so I figured that, because of the more sophisticated elements around them, the cowboys would have developed certain tastes for the better things in life, including, say, chunky vegetable chili, moist corn bread, and amusing little maple-pecan caramel crisps. It was what I served them on that first historic day, assuming that a low-fat, low-cholesterol kind of meal was what health-conscious Topangans would prefer over pork chops and spuds. I was wrong.

They wanted burgers or pizza or a meaty chili that a guy could actually, you know, chew while swilling his beer, not the prissy kinds of nibble-food found at tea parties and chamber-music recitals. Think back to the days when Clara Peller was shouting "Where's the beef?" on national television, add a dozen deep male voices to the chorus, and you'll have an echo of the response to my chunky vegetable chili. It wasn't a positive one.

"The problem," my wife said later, "is that you are not cooking for, well, ordinary people on a day of brain-smashing sport. These are not, after all, professors of Runic prose or poets of the haiku school. These are guys who, but for their wives, might be eating from bowls on the floor. So forget the wispy vegetarian chili and the neat little bar cookies. Go for the gusto, Mac!"

Her reference to Mac reminded me that I was a Marine for two splendid years of mud and grime and people shooting at me, so surely there ought to be something in that history to suggest the kinds of chow that real men liked. Unfortunately, however, the only items I can recall from that brief tour of duty are a cold, greasy hash eaten from a C-ration can and a pale, creamy chipped beef on toast that carried a description it is not possible to repeat in this format. And then it dawned on me: I would cook my famous pasta.

Well, actually, it isn't famous outside the family and a few friends, but everyone seems to like it, so I cook it whenever I am depressed, which is often. I use linguini as the pasta and fix a puttanesca sauce, which I am shy to say, is also known as a "whore's sauce" in the world of cookery. It contains pretty much what you want it to contain, including beer or a cheap red wine, but I leave out the alcohol, because I don't want my little grandchildren staggering away from the dinner table singing sailor songs.

Basically, the sauce, which I prepare in the morning and allow to simmer all day, consists of ground beef, cans of diced tomatoes, freshly chopped onions, garlic, oregano, capers, black olives, and two packets of prepared spaghetti spices. I don't usually mention that because purists dislike anything prepackaged but inasmuch as this is for football fans and not gourmet cooks, who cares? I served it the year the New York Giants beat Buffalo 20-19, and because it was one hell of a game, the human descendants of Pavlov's dog who ate my pasta associate it with pleasure and therefore recall the meal with a certain fondness, the way a man remembers the first duck he shot.

Speaking of which, for a while I considered a recipe for duck I had come across in a French cookbook, before I realized that French cooking probably was not what the boys in the living room would prefer. The recipe called for acquiring a live duck and smothering it so that the blood would congeal inside the bird, thereby making it more, well, succulent. But despite my tenure as a U.S. Marine, I have no training in smothering ducks. I did, however, mention it to a former Green Beret who was to be a guest of my Super Bowl blowout. He said that while he didn't particularly like duck, he wouldn't mind smothering one, which offers flashing insight into the moral imperatives associated with those I invited over. I served a pot roast instead that year. No one had to smother the cow.

I mention all this, I suppose, to emphasize the importance of tradition on Super Bowl Sunday. It varies from place to place, but let me assure you that in San Diego, where many Navy and Marine veterans abide, they are more oriented toward red meat than tuna salads. In other areas of southern California, most notably Malibu and La Jolla, you will find pockets of those who prefer bottled water to bottled beer and watercress sandwiches on six-grain bread to buffalo ribs, but the likelihood is they will be watching Japanese samurai movies on videotape and not the Super Bowl.

Notwithstanding the absent intelligentsia, crowding around the old television set on Super Bowl Sunday is not only an American tradition but a global one, too. While an estimated 150 million viewers in this country see The Game, another 700 million also see it worldwide. There are no statistics relating to other galaxies, but one must assume they see it out there, too. The popularity of the game, I mean The Game, became clear when it was observed in 1970 that more people watched Kansas City beat Minnesota 23-7 than watched American astronaut Neil Armstrong walk on the moon the year before. The lunar landing, I guess, may have been a giant step for mankind but it wasn't Len Dawson leading the Chiefs to victory.

My concern as I write weeks in advance of Super Bowl Sunday remains, as always, what to serve the boys clustered around my television set on the day of The Game. This has been going on, more or less, for about eight years, and while they're appreciative of my pasta, I think they're tired of it. I hear a low growling as they chow down. From some mammals, the primitive snarl might indicate contentment, but from the guys who watch football this is not a positive sound.

I'm thinking of grilling steaks for Super Bowl XXXII on the theory that a good chunk of meat will soothe any carnivore, the way the carcass of an impala satisfies a lion. He does not actually have to be eating it, just having it near offers a certain comfort. Perhaps I will cook the steaks, hide them, and let my guests sniff them out. They can bring the meat back in their teeth to either eat or just hug while they swill their beer, yell, hoot, holler, and bark until The Game has ended. And to hell with those amusing little maple-pecan caramel crisps.

JACK KEMP

BLACK AND WHITE

On the football field, the differences of race,
creed, and class are dissolved in the common
struggle for the end zone

FROM SUPER BOWL XXXII

G ROWING UP IN LOS ANGELES in the 1940s and 1950s, my
dream was to be a professional football quarterback. I
went to my first pro football game at 12, when the Los Angeles Rams were playing in the Coliseum. As I watched, I
dreamed of one day playing on the same field as my boyhood heroes, quarterbacks Bob Waterfield and Norm Van Brocklin and
halfback Kenny Washington, who became the first African-American to play in the NFL in 13 years.

I was drafted out of Occidental College in 1957 by the Detroit Lions. I was a seventeenth-round pick, but it didn't matter. I was
thrilled just to have a chance to play in the NFL for a team coached
by the legendary Buddy Parker and quarterbacked by the remarkable Bobby Layne. Not only had I begun to fulfill a lifelong vision,
but I also had the satisfaction of knowing that years of hard work,

training, and practice had paid some satisfying dividends.

Playing football taught me that nothing great happens without discipline, inspiration, and perspiration. My inspiration came one memorable day as a freshman at Occidental. Our freshman football coach, Payton Jordan, called me into his office and told me—confidentially—that if I worked hard and never gave up, I could reach the NFL some day. I walked out of his office on cloud nine and practiced harder than ever.

Years later, I learned that Coach Jordan had the same "confidential" conversation with many of his other players, including Ron Botchan and Jim Mora. Nevertheless, he inspired me and many others to live up to our God-given potential and never to give up on our dreams.

Playing professional football was my shot. Through the game, I learned that the opportunity always is there for anyone who is willing to put in the effort.

But during the course of my 13-year career in pro football, from 1957 to 1969, I could not avoid the harsh reality that in the 1950s and 1960s, the American Dream was only a distant hope for many of my African-American teammates and friends. Pro football had given many of us a magnificent opportunity, but other segments of America's society still were trapped in ignorant and hateful habits of thought and behavior that precluded all too many from being seen and treated as equals.

In 1961, when I was quarterback and captain of the San Diego Chargers, we were scheduled to play the Oilers in Houston for the AFL championship. Traditionally, the night before the game, coach Sid Gillman took the entire team to a movie. On this night, though, shortly after we sat down in our seats, I looked around and realized that some of my teammates were missing—players such as Paul Lowe, Ernie Ladd, and Charlie McNeil. I was told that they had been sent to the "blacks-only" balcony. When I told Coach Gillman, he immediately rounded up the players and we left the theater as a team, in a silent, but powerful, demonstration of our team's belief in racial equality.

Later, after I joined the Buffalo Bills, I had the honor of quarterbacking several AFL All-Star Games with players such as Ernie Warlick of the Bills, Abner Haynes of the Kansas City Chiefs, Art Powell of the Raiders, and Cookie Gilchrist of the Bills. At the AFL All-Star Game in New Orleans in January, 1965, my black teammates were unable to get taxis, decent accommodations, or even basic service at restaurants and nightspots because of the color of their skin.

In this case, it was the popularity of pro football that gave us the leverage needed to combat such discrimination incidents. In our team meeting we agreed to boycott the game because of the racial climate in the city. As a result the game was moved to Houston, which by that time had made progress toward equal treatment in public accommodations.

I don't bring this up to rekindle hard feelings, but to build on the lessons from sports and to recognize the legacy of the New South. These were men with whom I considered myself privileged to play the game, men who excelled at football and life. Yet they were held back because of their race. Their treatment flew in the face of our nation's ideals.

I am glad that, at least on the field, we did not struggle with the racial disparities that characterized American society during that decade. On the field, the differences of race, creed, and class were dissolved in the common struggle for the end zone. Artificial divisions had no place in a huddle.

The game of football, indeed all team sports, necessitates this unity. A team has to move in concert, each person understanding and assisting the roles of his teammates. If the team does not do this, it goes down in defeat. You win or lose as one team, one family, one unit. When a successful team walks onto the field, the issues of race and religion should be inconsequential. There is no room for racism, anti-Semitism, or prejudice.

I believe that is why team sports in general, and the NFL in particular, have been a vanguard of racial equality. Those who love to play the game well, and who respect the concept of the team, don't have room for such distractions.

That was the case in 1947 in professional baseball with Pee Wee

Reese, the Brooklyn Dodgers shortstop. When the Dodgers received word from Branch Rickey that they would be adding a new infielder named Jackie Robinson, many players circulated a petition stating they would not take the field with a black man. When Reese, the team captain, refused to sign the petition, he effectively put an end to the controversy.

But the influence of sports and athletic competition goes far beyond the sphere of the players to the millions of fans who love the game and admire the players.

In 1947, the fans regularly heckled, spat upon, and threw things at Jackie Robinson until finally, during a game in Cincinnati, Pee Wee walked over to his teammate, the first black player in the major leagues, and put his arm around him. Reese and Robinson stared down the crowd until the stadium was silent, then the game resumed. The power of one man doing the right thing at the right time is one of the greatest influences in our society.

Individually, we are not all captains of our own teams. But we are captains of our own souls. Just as collectively, we are the captain of the soul of our nation—and the soul of America is at stake in how we handle racial justice and reconciliation.

For me, the true model of leadership is the Good Shepherd, who left "the 99" to save one stray lamb. Ultimately, that has been the most valuable lesson of all—that our precious experiment in human justice and freedom will be judged on how we treat those who have been left out. America cannot lead the world to democracy, social justice, and free enterprise if we don't make those ideals work for all of our people here at home. I learned this firsthand during my 13 seasons of professional football, and I'm proud that my sons, Jeff and Jimmy, also carried those lessons into their professional football careers.

JAMES W. HALL

MAD MANNY

*It's difficult for a football fan to carry
a grudge when he and his enemy root
for the same team*

<small>FROM SUPER BOWL XXXIII</small>

M ANNY SHATNER WAS IN A FIX. Ten minutes till game time
and he couldn't get his helmet over his ears. Like his
head had swollen in the week since he'd worn it last.

Manny shook out his arms and set his cleats on the fresh sod,
hooked his fingers into the ear holes again and took a deep breath
and yanked. But the helmet only budged an inch. And now his
ears were twisted down and pressed so hard against the side of his
head it felt like any second his brains would erupt from the top of
his skull.

With a groan, he sat down in the recliner he'd set up in the visi-
tor's end zone. The floor of his living room was covered with natural turf, lined with lime. He'd designed everything to scale to fit
the twelve-by-twenty space. Seven-foot orange goal posts at each
end of the room, and a TV set perched between the uprights of

each one. A home-team TV, and one for the visitors. Manny changed ends at the end of each quarter.

To distract himself from the pain, Manny turned to the pregame show on the 40-inch TV at one end of the room. Next up were the Dolphins versus the Jets in New York. Winner got home-field advantage for the playoffs. Loser had to play the Patriots in the first round. The Dolphins hadn't beaten the Patriots for two years.

Manny Shatner went to all the Dolphins' home games. He always wore his aquamarine Lycra stretch suit, goofy orange sunglasses, and a rubber helmet shaped like Flipper. He had great seats on the 50-yard line, section 214, a 10-year license, hundred and twenty bucks a game. But the truth was, he did not actually use his seat much. He spent maybe half the game wandering up and down the aisles, rooting and exhorting. Pumping his arms like a pelican trying to take off.

He was known as Mad Manny the Dolphin Guy. He'd been on TV a lot. Local and national, been on *Monday Night Football* twice. He'd even been interviewed by one of the *Good Morning America* people a few years ago.

Sure, there were people who thought he was nuts. But Manny didn't mind. He was an entertainer. Made people smile. That was his mission in life, what kept him going.

But Manny didn't fly, hated taxis, hotel rooms, all of that. So he didn't go to the away games. Instead, he set up the simulated field in his living room. Grass and goal posts and each of the walls painted with scenes from Pro Player Stadium, detailed images of the stands packed with screaming fans. Manny did the painting. That was his occupation. He was a house painter. Worked for his landlord, Juan Fallad. He thought he'd done a damn good job on the painting in his living room, though he'd never shown it to anybody.

The helmet was killing him. Pinching his ears, scrambling his thoughts, probably cutting off the blood to some crucial part of his brain. He could pull the thing off and watch the game bareheaded. Nobody would ever know. But Manny had standards. And he was superstitious, too. If he didn't wear the rubber Flipper helmet

MAD MANNY

and the Dolphins ended up losing, he'd never forgive himself.

So while the network went to commercial, the kickoff just three minutes away, Manny stood up and marched across the grass field to the side wall where he'd painted the north side of the stadium, his own section. He lowered his head, then tipped it up again to check the distance. One good head butt ought to do it.

He rushed the wall. Threw himself into the plaster. Locked his neck tight, and hit that wall with his whole 268 pounds. He felt the jolt, felt the helmet settle snugly into place. Then Manny saw the lights flicker, heard a long woosh, and he was gone.

"What happened to him?" Rafael stood in the doorway staring at the body in the aquamarine suit sprawled on the living room grass.

"He looks dead," Sheila whispered.

"What's with all this grass?"

Rafael gestured at the expanse, then looked over his shoulder at the door he had just jimmied.

"Guy's crazy. I told you."

Sheila was 19, slim and tall with candy-corn tinted hair. She was wearing pink leotards and an orange blouse, chrome wraparound sunglasses. A Miami girl. Flashy and out there. Rafael had on jeans and a T-shirt and flip-flops. He was 20 and worked at a car wash, pulling down almost what Sheila did as a roller-skating waitress at the Steak n Shake.

She lived two doors down from Manny Shatner in a duplex, and she'd peeked in Mad Manny's house a few times and seen the grass on his floor and the goal posts and the two TVs.

She and Rafael were just starting out in the burglary business. Five houses so far. Something they did on weekends. It was sort of a hobby.

"Think we should call 911?" Rafael was stooped over the body, touching a finger to the gray rubber of Mad Manny's Flipper helmet.

"Call 911 and do what, tell the cops we just wandered into this place?"

182

"Guy's had a heart attack or something. He's dying."

"So give him mouth to mouth, Rafe. Get down and blow air into him."

Rafael was looking up at one of the TV sets. The Dolphins were losing 28-14 and punting from deep in their own territory.

"Those are nice televisions," he said. "And big."

Sheila smiled.

"You get busy with them," she said. "I'll look around, see if there's anything else."

"Somebody stole your season tickets?"

The young cop was standing in the middle of the living room taking Manny's statement. His older partner had kneeled down poking a finger in the turf.

Manny lifted his throbbing head from his hands.

"Yeah, they went in my drawer and took my tickets. All of them."

"This real grass?" the old cop said.

"Prescription Athletic Turf," Manny told him. "Same as they have at Pro Player."

The cops looked at each other. The young one looked serious. The old one grinned like an idiot.

From his headbutt, Manny had gotten the helmet on. But now he was worried it would never come off.

"Two televisions and season tickets to the Dolphins."

"That's right."

"You got an estimated value?"

Manny looked up at the young cop. The helmet was pinching his ears like crazy. They were still twisted under. When he finally got the helmet off he was going to look like Dumbo for the rest of his life.

"Estimated value on the tickets?" the cop said again.

Manny stared at him.

"Priceless," Manny said. "Incalculable."

Manny turned his head and saw Juan Fallad, his landlord and boss, standing in the open door. Fallad had never been in his house before, never seen the grass.

MAD MANNY

"Pack your stuff, Shatner," Juan Fallad said. "And be outta my house by sundown. You're bananas—a nut case. And don't bother coming into work tomorrow either, or the day after that."

The woman in the ticket office at Pro Player listened to Manny's story about his stolen tickets.

"Happens every day of the week," she said. She handed him new tickets for his seat. Printed across each ticket was the word "Duplicate."

"And if someone tries to use my real tickets?"

"You inform security and they'll be escorted from the stadium."

"You don't arrest them?"

"It never sticks. They say they got the tickets from their cousin's next-door neighbor. No way to prove they actually stole them."

"Escort them from the stadium. That's all you do?"

The woman took another look at Manny's ears. Just like he'd feared, they were flared out from being bent double for so long. Dumbo the Dolphin Guy.

"That's all we can do," she said. She looked over his shoulder at the guy in line behind him.

"Well, then," Manny said. "I guess I'll have to take care of it myself."

"They'll arrest you," Rafael said.

"No, they won't." Sheila was putting the last touches on her makeup, staring at the mirror in the bathroom of her duplex.

"You don't even like football."

"But these are great seats. Friend of mine who works in a sports bar says they're on the fifty-yard line, close to the field."

"This is nuts, you going to a football game. Sunday's our burglary day."

Sheila finished with the blue eye shadow and turned on Rafael. He was standing there in his underwear, watching her.

"You could scalp those tickets, Sheila, make a couple hundred bucks."

"Couple hundred bucks, huh? A week from now it's dribbled between our fingers, we got nothing to show for it."

"What're you gonna have to show from going to some football game?"

"I don't know," she said. "Ask me tonight."

Manny fondled the two-shot derringer inside his jacket pocket as he walked through the turnstile. It was almost as if he had to reassure himself that it still was there.

Quickly, he found the section where his seat was located.

Manny recognized her right away. Her name was Sheila. She lived down the block from him and hung out with some loser named Rafael. She was sitting in Manny's seat. Not cheering, not standing up when the Dolphins completed a pass. Not booing the hated Patriots.

Manny went about his super fan routines, roaming the aisles. He moved up and down the stairs blowing his kazoo, shaking the New England Patriot effigy doll, getting some cheers and some laughs. With less than two minutes left in the fourth quarter, Manny still hadn't confronted Sheila. Dolphins with the ball, down by seven. Whole season on the line.

Manny had known Sheila's parents, a couple from Ohio, hard workers. Died within six months of each other. Cancer, heart attack. Sheila dropped out of high school, lived in the house where she'd grown up. Then she started running with Rafael.

Manny watched her sitting there in his seat. Sheila never moved. Just sat there eating from a bag of peanuts and watching the game like she didn't understand what was going on.

Manny moved down the aisle. People yelled at him. Mad Manny the Dolphin Guy. Hey, Mad Manny. Strangle that Patriot. Manny turned around, held up the effigy and shook it hard.

He had the derringer hidden in his right hand.

Manny's seat was just two in from the aisle.

With 15 seconds left, Marino hit his tight end in the end zone. Time out. Coach Johnson was going to go for the two-point conversion, the win, not the tie. Everybody in Pro Player stadium was standing.

MAD MANNY

If he was going to shoot her, now was the time. Manny moved down the aisle. He had lost his house, his job, two expensive TVs.

The Dolphins were lined up for the two-point conversion. Everyone in the stadium was screaming. Mad Manny slid down the aisle, crowded in behind Sheila.

The ball was snapped. Marino faked a handoff down the middle and bootlegged. Gimpy, slow, Marino loped around left end. Nothing anyone would have expected. Just one giant defensive end between him and the goal line.

For a half-second there was silence. Utter, absolute quiet. Then a roar.

Sheila was climbing up on Manny's seat. She pumped both arms up in the air as if she were about to start an aerobics routine. It didn't matter that she didn't know the rules or what was at stake. The game had swept her up.

As Marino dived for the goal line, Sheila and Manny both screamed. Their voices found a seam in the air, a narrow slit in the chaos of the moment, rising above all the other voices.

Sheila jumped. Marino hit the end zone.

Mad Manny the Dolphin Guy bowed his head, and put his gun away.

It was her seat now. For as long as she wanted it.

LETTERMAN'S NFL SCRAPBOOK

You don't think there's anything funny

about football? You haven't heard what

The Late Show *host has to say*

FROM SUPER BOWL XXXV

N
O ONE IS BETTER AT COMPILING lists than comedian David Letterman, who punctuates the *Late Show With David Letterman* on CBS with a distinctive Top 10. Following is a special Top 10 created just for Super Bowl XXXV, plus some excerpts from his football-related lists and monologues.

Top 10 signs that your team won't be winning the Super Bowl
10. You suffer a groin pull during the coin toss.
 9. Players promise to go out and give 42 percent.
 8. Your quarterback leaves after the third quarter to "beat the traffic."
 7. Team's playbook drawn on Arby's napkin.
 6. The cheerleaders consist of two fat guys and the coach's mom.

5. Your team is made up of the finest football players Belgium has to offer.

4. Dennis Miller decides you're not worthy of an incomprehensible simile.

3. Team's last win came against the Baltimore Colts.

2. Your logo is Richard Simmons.

And the number-one sign your team won't be winning the Super Bowl...

1. People from Florida are keeping track of the number of points scored.

Ways to Mispronounce Vinny Testaverde
Tinny Vestaroody
Voonie Testaviddy
Wind-Tested Furby
Danny Bonaduce
Doug Flutie

Signs You're at a Bad Super Bowl Party
• Only snack is a tattered pack of lemon-honey throat lozenges.
• The TV is off, the disco is blaring, and everybody's wearing leather.
• Host serves the sandwiches by hiking them between his legs.
• You know that eye black the players wear? They're serving it on Wheat Thins.
• Host can't go out for more beer because of electronic ankle bracelet.

Punch Lines to Dirty Football Jokes
"No—I said, 'Look at the size of Mike Ditka.'"
"Next time, moisten the needle before inflating."
"She thought it was Jimmy Johnson's hair."
"For God's sake, don't spike it."
"Dick Butkus."
"And then the Viking nailed the Cowboy from behind."

DAVID LETTERMAN

Signs Your NFL Team Won't Do Well This Season
- Coach refers to Xs and Os as kisses and hugs.
- Instead of cooler of Gatorade, giant blender of margaritas.
- Team's only playoff experience was in the Betty Crocker bake-off.
- Team's new cheer includes "rebuilding season."
- The players have gained so much weight they don't need pads in their uniforms.

Dallas Cowboys Cheerleaders' Pet Peeves
- Being charged by the airline for an extra seat for all of our hair.
- Getting in line at the concession stand behind John Madden.
- When Troy Aikman has a concussion and keeps calling you Larry.
- When you step in the stadium nacho cheese sauce and have to throw away your boots.
- Carpal tunnel pompon syndrome.
- After the crowd gives you a "C"and an "O" and a "W" and a "B" and an "O" and a "Y" and an "S" and you ask them what they have and they don't know.

Things You Don't Want to Hear in a Huddle
"Immigration just hauled off our kicker."
"Hold me."
"I think you're using my mouthpiece."
"Did I show you guys the complete line of Amway products yet?"
"You think that's a groin pull—take a look at this."

Least Inspirational Things For a Coach to Say at Halftime
"If you don't mind, I'm leaving now for another appointment."
"They may have the talent, size, and athleticism—but we got the headbands."
"Who's winning?"
"I just won Powerball. So long, suckers!"

LETTERMAN'S NFL SCRAPBOOK

Selected offerings from past Letterman monologues:

New Year's Eve in New York City in Times Square is really unbelievable...it's like hundreds of thousands of drunks down there
gathered around to watch them drop a ball. It's like a Giants'
game.

What a crazy weekend! Here's what you had: Of course, you had
the war in Iraq that was going on...then, of course, you had the impeachment going on. That was a pretty big deal. And, of course,
the big game with the Jets on Saturday. And it's possible, when
you're trying to concentrate on all three of these events and run
your own life that you can become confused, and for a time, this
was my impression of what had happened: Congress voted two articles of impeachment, but voted down instant replay.

Over the weekend, the New York Jets and New York Giants both
lost. If you saw the games, you know that the Jets did not play very
well and the Giants did not play very well. But, in their defense, I
think they were still in shock from winning the week before.

I want to take a second here to congratulate the Green Bay Packers for winning, and also I want to congratulate the New England
Patriots for having fans who don't wear food on their heads.

I think the Pack is back, and I think that the people here in New
York City are still excited about the Packers' Super Bowl victory.
This morning, coming to work, my cab driver—honest to God—
was wearing a cheese turban.

You don't have to have a big Super Bowl party to enjoy yourself.
Here's what I do every Super Sunday. I tip the Domino's guy five
bucks, and then he stays and watches the first half with me.

Here's what I want to say about this snowball-throwing incident at
Giants Stadium. It was ugly, it was embarrassing, they shouldn't

really be doing that. On the other hand, it was nice to see someone finally hitting the Giants' receivers.

There's something magic about Christmas in New York City...It would have been a great holiday—till my mom got arrested for disorderly conduct at Giants Stadium.

JIM MURRAY

TOO LITTLE, TOO LATE

Lovable Art Rooney waited a long
time for a championship, but he was
far too nice to grow impatient

FROM SUPER BOWL XXXIII

Jim Murray, a Pulitzer prize-winning columnist, entertained readers of
the Los Angeles Times *for 37 years. Some classic excerpts:*

There's an old George M. Cohan song that goes "Aitch-ay-dooble-are-eye-gee-ay-en spells 'Harrigan.' Proud of all of the Irish blood that's in me. Divil a man can say word agin me."

Except for a change in spelling, that song could apply to Arthur J. Rooney, owner of the best damned football team in the universe.

Art Rooney is a man without an enemy. Friend of man, Irish to the core, a sucker for a hand out, he has gone through life like a parish priest in the Bowery. He made a million bucks, but never became lace-curtain Irish in his life. An amiable drinker, never a drunk, he was the one to help his friends home.

He's probably the only man in the Pittsburgh Steelers' organization today who feels sorry for the Minnesota Vikings. If he had his way, he'd probably trade L.C. Greenwood or Franco Harris to them tomorrow. He's done it all his life.

He almost seemed disappointed to win. Art Rooney is a man who would much rather lose himself than have his friends do it. After all, he's used to it.

The only place he has never lost is at the racetrack. Horses have never let him down. Plenty of humans have. He always forgave them.

"They think I won this team at Saratoga," he was saying the other day, after he had delayed his arrival at Super Bowl IX for several days because he didn't want to upstage the team. "I'll tell you fellows the truth on that. I did have a good day at Saratoga once, and the columnist, Bill Corum, was with me and betting with me. The next day, he wrote a piece about the killing we made. I was like the guy who broke the bank at Monte Carlo, and it was a good story. So the next day the Hearst papers assigned a man to follow me around. He did. And we lost quite a few races, too. But he kept writing that we didn't. 'I can't write about a loser,' he told me, 'and I like this assignment too much.'"

For Art Rooney, the Super Bowl championship is like so many things that happen to us in life—too late and too empty. Winning is a young man's game. Winning is not for men who remember Bullet Bill Dudley and Whizzer White and Johnny Blood. Winning is not for men who look at all those muscular young strangers and wonder where Fats Henry and Bronko Nagurski have gone. Winning is not nostalgic when all the winners are bulls young enough to be your great-grandchildren.

Winning is for people who can drink the champagne and stay up all night on Bourbon Street. Winning is not for people who have to go home and have a glass of warm milk and a good cry because things are not really the same any more.

Winning is beating George Halas or Wellington Mara or Curly Lambeau, not some Minneapolis corporation.

Winning was for the days when you showed up in New Kensington, Pennsylvania, and the promoter couldn't come up with a guarantee, so you didn't put your team on the field till he paid off in hot dogs or hogs. Winning was for the days when checks bounced, and you would pay a man like Mean Joe Greene $100 a game, not $100,000 a season.

"What does 'winning' mean to me?" a puzzled Art Rooney, an old man with cataracts and balloon glasses now, not the pompadoured dandy who broke the books at Saratoga so many years ago in the Great Depression, asked. "Well, I'll tell you. First, I feel sorry for guys like Well Mara and George Halas, my pals, who haven't won in a long time. We went through some hard times in this business.

"I remember young Terry Bradshaw came into my office one day about something and I said, 'Terry, what would you do if the lights went out?' And he said, 'What?' and I said, 'What if they turned those television lights out? Would you play for $15,000 a season like Whizzer White? Would you if we had to put the team back in the bus and mark out a football field someplace and pass the hat?'"

Bradshaw's answer was not recorded, but it's clear that Art Rooney was not looking at the 1975 Super Bowl, which is Roman numerated, as Red Smith says, like Popes. He was looking at Wrigley Field in 1933 or the Polo Grounds in 1935. He was wondering where Ken Strong went, or Tuffy Leemans or Beattie Feathers.

Jimmy Cagney, the great actor, was once asked to describe the Irish in one word, and he came up with "malice."

But Art Rooney doesn't have a malicious bone in his body. He is as softhearted as a monsignor in a leper colony. He flew in for the game everybody who ever came to him for a loan or a job. He flew in his home-field ground crew, the people who serve drinks.

It's a good thing Minnesota didn't ask for the game back. Art Rooney would have given it to them.

It took 42 years, but the hundred-to-one shot finally came in. If it hadn't, Art Rooney would have shrugged, lit a cigar, and gone and bought somebody a drink. He's bet on lots of also-rans before. He's never been known to say "if we had only...." or to fault the writer, the officials, or the team, or the fates. His team was lousy because he could never bear to fire anybody. He once fired Johnny Blood, and Johnny Blood stayed on anyway.

For Art Rooney, it's too little and too late. He was the least-excited man in New Orleans. A scoreless tie would have suited him fine. He wasn't looking at coach Chuck Noll out there. He was looking at Jock Sutherland in 1947. That was the very good year, not 1975. Like finally getting a girl you brought flowers to 35 years ago.

But, for Art Rooney, he'll go through the motions. He hates to hurt people's feelings. His philosophy is very simple: "I'll tell you," he said, flicking an unlit cigar the other day, "if you don't like people, you get the worst of it." (Super Bowl IX)

THE MOUSE ROARED

First of all, are you sitting down?

Be sure who you tell this to or they'll think you've been drinking.

On Sunday afternoon, the canary ate the cat. The mailman bit the police dog. The minnow chased the shark out of its waters. The missionaries swallowed the cannibals. The rowboat rammed the battleship. The mouse roared, and the lion jumped up on a chair and began to scream for help.

The first thing that's going to surprise you about the Super Bowl is the closeness of the score. But, hang on to your hat. If you think that's a shocker, wait till I get to the punch line.

The—come closer and let me whisper this—New York Jets are the Super Bowl champions of football! Cross my heart! That funny little team from that funny little league they left on pro football's doorstep a few years back. You know the one—the team whose checks bounced and so did their quarterbacks.

They said (Norman Van Brocklin did) that Broadway Joe would be playing in his first professional game in the Super Bowl. Well, he likes it better than that game they play over in that other league. He got beat three times in that league.

They said the Jets were the third-best team in their own league. If so, it's a good thing they didn't send the best. Everybody would have switched over to Heidi. (Super Bowl III)

TOO LITTLE, TOO LATE

LOMBARDI SAID, 'HO, HO, HO!'

No, Virginia, there is no Santa Claus. They pulled his whiskers off at the Coliseum Sunday and it turned out to be Vince Lombardi saying "Ho, ho, ho!"

Sorry, kids, fairy tales don't come true, after all. Sleeping Beauty was really dead. Hansel and Gretel never did get out of the oven. The giant ate Jack and the beanstalk.

Little Red Riding Hood didn't notice Grandma's ears 'til too late, and she found out her teeth were too big the hard way. Goldilocks is just a big lie.

All of which is my way of telling you the clock struck midnight for the American Football League Sunday. Brute strength conquered in the end again. They played for money and them that has, got. (Super Bowl I)

LOSERS LOSE

Well, I guess it's safe to throw away your Stassen buttons. And burn your Confederate money. Losers lose.

The Minnesota Vikings lost a Super Bowl Sunday. And the sun rises in the East and Elizabeth Taylor gets married.

One more of these and the AFC gets the Minnesota Vikings stuffed and put on their wall in the den.

Minnesota showed a lot of guts showing up. Next time, they get to mail the loss in.

The NFC should keep an understudy standing in the wings when the Vikings go into their act. If an act like theirs played the Palace, they'd get pelted with tomatoes.

If they're going to play it for comedy, shouldn't they come out in baggy pants with a seltzer bottle and Groucho Marx mustaches? In fact, the Minnesota teams should sell the routine to the Marx Brothers. Their defensive line is funnier than Chaplin.

The knock against the Vikings' Fran Tarkenton is that he-can't-throw-the-long-one, but he threw a 75-yard touchdown pass in this game. Unfortunately, it was to Oakland. (Super Bowl XI)

HAROLD ROSENTHAL

THE GOOD OLD DAZE

Once upon a time, the Super Bowl was just another game, and the foibles surrounding it almost outnumbered the fans

FROM SUPER BOWL XXXII

I T SAYS HERE THAT the first Super Bowl was the most important football game ever played. If that initial effort flopped because of box-office failure, mutual distrust between the AFL and NFL, or the inability of the bus drivers to find their way over to the Los Angeles Coliseum from downtown headquarters at Seventh and Figueroa, January might as well be missing one Sunday.

There would be no Super Sunday (nor would there be such excuses as "I'm sorry, I'm flying out to the Super Bowl with the secretary-general," or "Better call nine-one-one. I can't do much about that water coming through the ceiling until this half ends").

They played that epochal game (a) with one seat in every three unoccupied and (b) virtually under an alias. In the interval between the early June, 1966 merger announcement and the January 15, 1967 confrontation between the AFL and NFL, designers labored to fit the typographical legend "AFL-NFL World Championship Game" onto a standard-sized ticket without making it look and read like a disheartened double-acrostic.

Years later, when "Super Bowl" rolled off the tongue as if it had been that forever, Pete Rozelle was asked a late-evening question. How come it was AFL-NFL World Championship Game rather than the other way around? Didn't the NFL have 15 clubs to the AFL's 9? And didn't NFL teams play in bigger cities?

Rozelle, who had a tremendous reputation for diplomacy and conciliation, took a thoughtful sip and suggested, "Alphabetical?"

Game II still was the AFL-NFL World Championship Game but the Orange Bowl was packed for a Green Bay repeat. For III, "Super Bowl" was on the cover of the game program, but not on the labels, note pads, and checks. Clearly progress was being made. The television people unabashedly referred to it as "Super Bowl." So did the newspapermen, who occasionally have been know to set tastes and standards. And for Game IV, it was official, and Lamar Hunt's daughter firmly was established in football history.

The Kansas City owner has told the story many times, about his little girl proudly showing off her high-bouncing ball and saying, "Look Daddy, my Super Ball," and Daddy responding with, "Don't let that kid out of the room without signing an agreement."

Actually, "Super Ball" is a trademark, and it says so in Webster's Collegiate Dictionary. Also in the current edition is "Super Bowl" with a 1969 "first-usage." It's defined as "a contest or event that is the most important or prestigious of its kind." In other words, it's correct to describe something as the "Super Bowl of Tiddlywinks," though it won't bring the same fees for television commercials.

All Super Bowls are special, but the first had something for posterity: real, live rocket men who traveled through space via propulsion from rocket units strapped to their backs. They soared to the rim of the Coliseum, made a circuit of the stadium, and returned to the 50-yard line. No one in the crowd ever had seen anything like it.

The first five Super Bowls were played in three cities: Los Angeles, Miami, and New Orleans. The prime concerns were warm weather and outdoor seating capacity. The Orange Bowl was the choice for numbers II and III, with New Orleans getting the nod for IV. The site was Tulane's capacious Tulane Stadium (home of the Sugar Bowl), and it was one of the coldest weeks in Creole memory.

Fountains are important in New Orleans, and the Kansas City club was quartered at a hotel that had fountains running out front, except they weren't doing that when the Chiefs arrived. The fountains unfroze just about game time, when a tornado watch had replaced the fourth day of rain.

Game IV marked my second year as the AFL public-relations man after a lifetime of newspapering. It was to prove a final victory before everything changed from "League" to "Conference." Kansas City whipped the Vikings thoroughly, causing Hank Stram, the Chiefs' coach, to interject gleefully into an open mike from NFL Films his evaluation of Minnesota's inability to cope on defense. "Hey," Stram shouted, "they're running around like a Chinese fire drill." Harmless then, politically incorrect today.

Earlier, Game IV had all the possibilities of a real two-alarm fire, and not without casualties, either. The pregame show included plans for two balloon ascensions, in costume. One of the basketeers, the one made up to resemble a horned Viking, revved up his three-foot long stream of plumber's torch flame, and prepared to ascend. The elements had other ideas, however, and a gust blew him across the field, where he landed against a barrier of cyclone fence. It was all that stood between the runaway monster and disaster for those in the seats.

In the seats were some of the crinolined ladies slated to participate in the halftime pageant. One was so frightened she suffered a broken leg while scrambling to safety.

The other guy in a balloon, rigged out as a bonneted Indian chief, then jumped out of his still-grounded basket, waved to the ground crew, and caught a cab back to the hotel. Just like in World War II, stars departed, and the ground crew cleaned up.

At halftime the wraps came off the ladies and a mob of uniformed participants in a re-enactment of the Battle of New Orleans. The ladies clambered into a period coach (actually it was a gussied up flat-bed truck) and off they went—for about five yards, until they sank hub-deep in the Louisiana gumbo. No one remembered it had rained for a week. They never made center stage.

So, the battle went on, with the Americans led by Old Hickory, still seen on the $20 bill, and opposed by some haughty Brit. Neither was aware the War of 1812 had been called off two weeks earlier (that's an historical fact; poor local delivery).

There was cannon fire, musket fire, and lots and lots of smoke.

The battle came to a sudden, unscheduled end. And onto the field rushed several real-life medics to minister to a fallen soldier who hadn't gotten up with the rest of the killed and wounded. This one just lay there holding his hand.

And well he should have. He had shot off one of his fingers.

Thirty years later, Don Weiss, former NFL executive director and senior surviving member of those early Super Bowl planners, was asked how one loses a finger while shooting blanks? "They wanted the sound real loud so they used extra-strength percussion caps," Weiss says.

Also that year, Pat O'Brien had an aching ear. O'Brien was a cherished Hollywood personality, welcomed in all sports crowds. His voice was unforgettable, whether giving Jimmy Cagney direction as the padre in the *The Fighting 69th*, or as Knute Rockne, taking the death-bed testimony of Notre Dame superstar George Gipp (played by Ronald Reagan).

Someone figured it would be a great idea to have Pat recite "The Star-Spangled Banner." And his musical accompaniment was Doc Severinsen, Johnny Carson's nationally recognized music man and horn player. Al Hirt, New Orleans's own trumpeter, had done some horn blowing in pregame ceremonies.

Pat and Doc shared a single microphone. It was a mistake. O'Brien faced it head-on; Severinsen had to come in from the side. His notes hit O'Brien's eardrum like a trip-hammer. And if O'Brien had pulled away he would have lost the mike. The sound system went out during the Anthem, and, when it came back on, Severinsen and O'Brien were not on the same page musically.

That afternoon Pat O'Brien joined the ranks of those who rate

"The Star-Spangled Banner" a "little long." As O'Brien said later, "I couldn't hear out of my right ear until the week before the Kentucky Derby."

Three years later (my last in the league office), the NFL returned to Los Angeles. Don Shula's Miami Dolphins were 16-0 (including the regular season and two playoff games) and amazingly were two-point underdogs to Washington. That was the game in which a field-goal attempt by Garo Yepremian, with the Dolphins leading 14-0, was blocked. Yepremian followed with a Buster Keaton routine by trying to pick it up and throw it to absolutely no one in particular. Instead, the Redskins' Mike Bass picked it off, went half the field with it, and it was a 14-7 game with two minutes left. Fortunately for Garo, that's also the way it ended.

This technical development is recalled only to update later generations on the gifted Yepremian's multilingual, multifaceted personality. Originally from Cyprus he was skilled in four languages, Greek, Turkish, English, and something else. In his down time, he had a tie-manufacturing business in Miami.

Super Bowl parties were very big with Pete Rozelle. The Super Bowl VII bash aboard the Queen Mary in Long Beach, California, was one of the biggest—and in very tight quarters.

And things got bigger and better with each game.

The best line to come out of any NFL party in my experience came from a gorgeous woman accompanying one of the mature New York tabloid columnists. At the festivities prior to Super Bowl VII, he was with this impressive young lady and had nowhere to sit. I had been protecting the last two seats at my table like an embattled bull elephant. This included rejecting a qualified owner whose club had had a 6-8 record that season. I ushered the columnist and his friend into these Tiffany spots, where the lady was introduced as "Ms. Brown."

Seated, the small talk was followed by the wine sipping, followed by toying with the appetizers, and then leaping into the 12-ounce steaks. We were about halfway home on the entrée when Ms. Brown turned to another woman and asked, "What is the name of the organization sponsoring this event?"

'V' AS IN VINCE,
'V' AS IN VICTORY

The NFL's most famous coach rode

his Green Bay Packers mercilessly,

and they loved him for it

FROM SUPER BOWL XXXIV

HERE IS A BLACK-AND-WHITE photograph of Vince Lombardi hanging in my office at NFL Films. My dad, Ed Sabol, gave it to me after we finished filming a 1968 television special about the Green Bay Packers. In the lower right corner of the photo is a hand-written message: "To Steve, a Schmuck If I Ever Saw One, Vince." Although that particular message probably was suggested to the coach by my father, the handwriting is Vince's. He enjoyed a good joke, and he loved to laugh.

He loved to win, too.

Nowhere—as a player at Fordham University, as the head coach at St. Cecilia High School in New Jersey, as an assistant coach at Army, as an assistant coach with the New York Giants, and then for nine years as head coach with Green Bay (where his teams won the first two Super Bowls) and for one last season as head coach of the Washington Redskins—did Vince Lombardi experience a losing season. His impact upon the game of football was so profound that his name was given to the greatest prize the game can offer—the Super Bowl trophy.

He has been characterized as a success-obsessed tyrant, a great leader, a butt-kicking bully who browbeat his players, a master motivator who drew out the best from his team. I knew him, and he was all of the above.

With many great coaches, it is the face that we remember—the jutting jaw of Don Shula, the frosty stare of Bud Grant, the scowl of Don Coryell. With Lombardi, it is different. How he looked ran second to how he sounded. It is in the ear of memory that he lingers. His voice was so unmistakable, so strident, so resonant, it could cut through anything. He could be on the other side of a room conversing in his normal tone, and everyone would hear him.

I was in Green Bay filming a morning practice session during summer camp. The players were doing calisthenics, with Ray Nitschke and Willie Davis leading the drills, when suddenly a little dog darted out of the crowd and onto the field. It pranced around, tail wagging, barking at the players who were trying unsuccessfully to shoo it away. A few fans were in the stands, and they were pointing and laughing. Then Lombardi appeared. He glared at the dog that was disrupting his practice and bellowed, "Get the hell off this field." The dog's tail dropped between its legs, and it scurried back into the crowd.

Vince Lombardi became head coach of the Packers in 1959 when he was 46 years old. He inherited a team that had lost 13 of its previous 15 games. There was no free agency then so he couldn't wheel and deal and create a new roster overnight. Instead, Lombardi made new players out of the ones he had. That was part of his genius.

His presence changed other men. "There's a gap between what you think you can do, and what you can actually do when you are motivated and inspired," former Packers guard Jerry Kramer says. "Lombardi felt it was his job to close that gap."

'V' AS IN VINCE, 'V' AS IN VICTORY

Lombardi rode his players mercilessly, and they loved him for it. They loved Lombardi because they won games.

The best evidence of Lombardi's skill as a molder of champions is a half-dozen players who were with the Packers before he arrived in Green Bay. In 1958, Paul Hornung, Jim Taylor, Jim Ringo, Bart Starr, Forrest Gregg, and Ray Nitschke were undistinguished members of the worst Packers team in history (1-10-1). All six now are in the Pro Football Hall of Fame. Lombardi transformed Hornung from a confused quarterback to a running back and kicker who set a record for most points (176) in a single season. He converted an ordinary fullback, Nitschke, into the finest middle linebacker in the NFL. And in Starr, a seventeenth-round draft choice from an Alabama team that won one game in Starr's senior year, Lombardi developed a brilliant quarterback.

He made them champions. He gave them a purpose. And a purpose is like a heart. You don't create a heart. But like the tin man in *The Wizard of Oz*, you can discover the one you always had.

Another Packers player who achieved Hall-of-Fame status under Lombardi was Henry Jordan. Of the hundreds of anecdotes that I've collected about Lombardi, Jordan gave me the most insightful analysis of his former coach. We were filming a documentary on Lombardi, and I was interviewing Jordan at his home. He said that there wasn't a day that went by that he didn't think about the coach and the values he instilled.

For 20 minutes, Jordan extolled Lombardi's humanity, generosity, and intelligence. When the interview was over, I had to go to the bathroom. He directed me to a small bathroom in the hallway. Directly opposite the toilet, hanging waist-high, was a photograph of Lombardi, just like the one my dad gave me.

When I returned to Jordan's living room I said, "After all the wonderful things you said about Coach Lombardi, why did you hang his picture opposite the toilet? That doesn't seem very respectful."

"I think it's very appropriate," Jordan responded. "That's the perfect place for Coach Lombardi's picture. If ever a man lived who could scare the crap out of you, he was the one!"

JIM KLOBUCHAR

THE CLASS OF 34

Walter Payton, a man of style and grace,

left a mark on pro football that was even

greater than his rushing record

FROM SUPER BOWL XXXIV

P RO FOOTBALL IS BIG and boisterous and sometimes brutal. It also is glamorous and rich and often heroic. And there are times when it is so big and visible it is simply engulfing. Pro football has earned all of those characterizations and more. One thing it rarely is called is beautiful. The game is about spectacle and the clash of powerful and driven men colliding with other powerful and driven men. But there are exceptions.

What happened in the hours following the death of Walter Payton though, transcended everything. The hours after Walter Payton died created for professional football players, coaches, and its followers a solidarity of grief and affection that seemed to wash away every conflict that divided them. It was an unforgettable moment.

Yes, he was a marvelous football player and a human being of decency and honor with streaks of intramural mischief. He was called all of that and more when he played and when he retired. But in the hours after he died November 1, Walter Payton did for football what his athletic skills and all of his records could not have done, what perhaps no other football player could have done.

In remembering who and what Payton was, pro football came together in a way that was spontaneous, passionate, and real. It cut across the whole range of the game's diversity. It brought together the men who had played with and against him, the coaches, younger players who knew him only through video flashbacks, and fans who only knew of his legend.

In these hours of mourning and celebration of his place in the game, pro football became a community again. These were the faces of pro football speaking from a hundred television studios and the multitudes of football watchers in front of their screens, bound in a remembrance of an extraordinary athlete and, more important, a good man. Little wonder that his nickname was "Sweetness," a tribute to his on-field and off-field style.

Communities don't have to last to the end of time. Sometimes they are united for a few hours or days. This one will last in the shared affection of that day. There will be other heroes but no one quite like him.

He was a football player whose death could reach a harsh and willful man such as Mike Ditka and touch him with humility. It could reach stoical and undemonstrative football men in the mold of Bud Grant and touch them with tenderness. It could reach an uncompromising competitor named Mike Singletary and touch him with peace.

What his friends and admirers saw in Walter Payton the day of his death, and what they tried to express, came down to this:

Walter Payton, as an athlete and as a role model, was about the best this game is ever going to produce. He made the others proud to share the fraternity of pro football with him. They were the men who played with him or against him, who could see his commitment on every play and in every game and in every side of his life. Being in the huddle with him, lining up with him, made them better. Gabbing in a café with him made the world a little lighter. Watching him struggle with his approaching death and hearing him say without melodrama that he would not give in made them grateful to know him. It made them believe there was a genuine, imperishable grace in how he played and lived.

"Walter played football the way nobody I'd ever seen," said Vikings defensive end Jim Marshall who squared off against Payton in the first five years of Walter's NFL career. "He just seemed invincible when he played. When he ran, he sprinted and juked and banged and did whatever he had to do to get an extra yard. He was an exuberant guy. He loved the world and the people he played with and his family. And you never think of a person like that as vulnerable. You think he'll just go on forever."

In some ways, he will.

THE NFL SUPER BOWL COMPANION
PERSONAL REFLECTIONS ON AMERICA'S FAVORITE GAME

Library of Congress Control Number: 2002109709

This book is available in quantity at special discounts for your group or organization.
For further information, contact:
TRIUMPH BOOKS
601 South LaSalle Street, Suite 500
Chicago, Illinois 60605
Phone (312) 939-3330 FAX (312) 663-3557

Printed in the United States of America

ISBN 1-57243-501-1

Editor-in-Chief	John Wiebusch
General Manager	Bill Barron
Executive Editor	Tom Barnidge
Managing Editor	John Fawaz
Senior Art Director	Sharon Peters
Associate Art Director	Sandy Gordon
Associate Editors	Joyce Cash, Joe Velazquez
Production Directors	Tina Dahl, Dick Falk